NEGOTIATE
AND
WIN

NEGOTIATE
AND
WIN

PROVEN STRATEGIES FROM THE NYPD'S
TOP HOSTAGE NEGOTIATOR

Dominick J. Misino
with Jim DeFelice

McGraw-Hill
New York   Chicago   San Francisco
Lisbon   London   Madrid   Mexico City   Milan
New Delhi   San Juan   Seoul   Singapore
Sydney   Toronto

The *McGraw·Hill* Companies

1 2 3 4 5 6 7 8 9 0   DOC/DOC   0 9 8 7 6 5 4

ISBN 0-07-142803-8

McGraw-Hill books are available at special quantity discounts to use as premiums and sales promotions, or for use in corporate training programs. For more information, please write to the Director of Special Sales, McGraw-Hill Professional, Two Penn Plaza, New York, NY 10121-2298. Or contact your local bookstore.

 This book is printed on recycled, acid-free paper containing a minimum of 50% recycled, de-inked fiber.

CONTENTS

CONTENTS

TALK TO ME

Any way you look at it, life is a negotiation. You go through a normal day, you're making twenty, thirty negotiations. Your wife wants you home for dinner, the boss wants you closing the big sale, the guy at the deli just bumped the price of coffee a quarter.

Sometimes the terms are pretty clear and the transaction is cut and dried: You're going to have to dig for that extra two bits or invest in a new Mr. Coffee. And most times the stakes aren't dire—though I, for one, wouldn't cross up my wife more than once a month, and even then I make sure I have the body armor on when I walk in the door. But whether your life is on the line or not, your success and happiness at any particular moment depends a great deal on your ability as a negotiator.

Now let me let you in on a little secret: You're already a pretty good negotiator. Hell, you're a born negotiator.

Seriously. See, in my opinion, everybody—everybody—can and does negotiate all the time. But for various reasons some of us fall into bad habits and traps and make a botch of it, at least some of the time.

Hey, I know. Happens to me all the time, and I do this stuff for a living.

In 1993, I found myself in the control tower at Kennedy Airport in New York City, speaking to a young man who called himself Jack. He was holding a pistol at the head of the pilot of Lufthansa Flight 592, an Airbus

310 with ninety-four passengers and ten crew members aboard flying toward New York. I was handed a note by an FBI agent that stated the hijacker had a list of demands that started with freeing every political prisoner in Bosnia. For all I know, he wanted to give Manhattan back to the Indians as well.

First thing I did was ball up his list of demands and toss them in the wastepaper basket. Then I asked him a simple question that somehow touched a nerve, and I had to listen to him harangue me for ten minutes.

About the only bright side to that was knowing that all the time he was screaming at me, he wasn't shooting anybody.

The question was: "What's your name?"

Talk about being sensitive. I mean really, you hijack a plane and want to land at the busiest airport in the world in drive time, you think you're going to be anonymous?

Tough start, but we got through it. A couple of million times while I was on the radio with him, things got touchy, but we did our dance—him at thirty thousand feet and me sitting there knowing that a hundred-plus lives were counting on my skills as a mouth warrior. And even though sometimes I think it might not be a horrible idea to give Manhattan back to *whoever* will take it, we did it without giving in to any of Jack's supposedly non-negotiable demands.

Hell, he even surrendered to me on the tarmac. Which would have been one of those warm and toasty memory moments except that it was so damn cold out there and he was carrying a backpack big enough to hold one very big bomb.

Some people you deal with want to blow your head off. Others are out to blow their own heads off—and take you out with them. But other people—with luck, *most* of the people you deal with—just want a good deal for themselves. They aren't interested in seeing you in pieces on the floor when they're done. That would only be a bonus.

In this book, we'll talk about all of those people, the good, the bad, the whacks. The techniques for dealing with them are basically the same; it's the tactics and expectations that shift a bit. The thing that doesn't change—that shouldn't change—is you. Any tactic, any stance or approach that you feel uncomfortable with, well, put it aside. Life is too short for you to feel uncomfortable looking yourself in the mirror at night. Besides, one of the most important parts of negotiating is feeling comfortable with yourself and your position. It comes through to the person you're negotiating with real quick. If you're not relaxed—if you're not confident and cool and comfortable—you won't pull it off.

And listen, being yourself works. Sometimes you just have to let it all hang out. Sometimes you have to just say, look, go ahead and jump if that's what you want to do.

That worked for me one night up on the Throgs Neck, which if you've ever been to New York, you know is a monster bridge. Of course, it worked because by then I had a good enough rapport with the guy that I knew he wasn't going to jump.

That, and my ninjas were positioned to grab him if he did.

Other times, all you have to do is take a step back.

One night while I was on duty with the NYPD hostage negotiation unit, we got a desperate call to head for the Whitestone Bridge. A jumper had climbed all the way up one of the towers. I won't bore you with my adventures getting there and my trek up the 250-foot ladder—I HATE bridge ladders, truly, and this night did not change my mind. But let me just say for now that I arrived on the scene somewhat miraculously, and even more incredibly, in one piece. Turned out I knew the would-be jumper—she was in the police department. So we're up there, got to be maybe 10 degrees below zero when you figure in the wind chill. We talk for a while and the subject doesn't want to come down, at least not the slow way.

Worse—she's nervous, real, real nervous. Which makes me nervous too. She's standing maybe three inches from the edge of the platform on the pier. Very easy to slip, especially if your knees are doing little fits.

So finally, I realize the reason she's nervous is probably not the height but the fact that my emergency services guys are within six or seven feet of her. They're close—but not quite close enough to grab her.

So what did I do?

I decided to be myself. I put it all on the line. "I'm nervous," I told her. Honest, no way I wasn't. Then I asked if she'd move back from the edge if we all moved back. Three feet for three feet.

No, she said.

I had everyone move back anyway. Then I told her that since we were all farther away, she had no reason to be close to the edge.

She thought about it. And thought about it. I waited. Finally, she took a step back from the edge. It wasn't an immense step, but it was definitely and absolutely in the right direction. And it was probably the hardest step for her to take. By giving a little, I gained a lot.

You don't have to play macho power games to succeed at negotiation. In fact, a lot of time those games are just a face-saving way of giving up. Hell, we can always storm the building. I used to be a sniper; I know how good the ninjas are.

But what's going to happen? Always, always, always, something you didn't predict. Oh, once in a while that's a good thing—heck, there *might* be a winning lottery ticket on the pavement in front of you, you never know. But a lot of times when negotiation fails, someone's going to get hurt. In my line of work, usually that someone is somebody I care about—a hostage, a ninja, even myself.

BUY THE TRUTH

People have a lot of misconceptions about negotiating. For one thing, they tend to see it as some exotic, mysterious art. Hey, I like to be considered exotic and mysterious as much as the next guy, but the truth is, negotiating is not rocket science, even if you do it for NASA. You can learn the basics by taking classes and reading books—mine included. You can get better at it by thinking about what you're doing, and by practicing.

Another big misconception—a huge misconception I run into all the time in my classes on hostage and business negotiation—is that negotiating is about fooling someone. Salesmen, who basically are negotiators, have a horrible reputation these days. Most people walking into a store or onto a car lot think they're going to be ripped off or somehow conned. I'm not saying that con artists don't exist, or that unscrupulous salesmen aren't out there—hey, I've dealt with them myself. But the attitude that you're going to be ripped off no matter what you do is self-defeating. It leads you not to do your homework properly, and it puts you in a frame of mind that isn't going to help you negotiate.

What you're doing is making yourself a victim. Ironic, isn't it? By thinking you're going to get screwed, you put yourself in a position where that may happen.

If, instead, you go in thinking you're going to find a solution to an issue—buying a car, negotiating a raise, finding health-care coverage you can live with—then you're on the road to reaching your goal.

Coming from the other direction, the customer's notion that he's going to be ripped off is often the salesman's biggest obstacle. Call it the fear factor or a siege mentality or a "me against the world" attitude; overcoming it is the key to a successful sale or negotiation. To break past it, you have to demonstrate concern and you have to be truthful. You sell the truth, not con the buyer or "mark."

Cops deal with the me-against-the-world attitude all the time. It's the first hurdle for a police department's hostage negotiator to overcome. He arrives on the scene with all these people pointing guns at each other and has to convince the guy inside that he's not going to get shot. It's not a con game—the subject won't be shot as long as he agrees to act a certain way. The negotiator is simply finding a way to sell the truth to that individual.

That's what the words "Talk to me" are all about.

THE BASICS, STEP-BY-STEP

As I travel around the country giving lectures and classes on hostage and business negotiating, I find a lot of similarities between the two. Now don't get me wrong—I'm not recommending you hire a SWAT team to back you up when you go to negotiate your next raise. But you *should* have what the SWAT team represents for a hostage negotiator: a viable alternative in the negotiations, even if it is not the best possible result.

What we're going to do in this book is walk through the basic outline of my program. We'll talk about hostage negotiation, real stuff from things I've been through, and we'll put it into play in "normal" situations, the kind of stuff you face every day. I'll show you how to use my approach when you buy your car or negotiate the family vacation. It'll be just like one of my seminars, except without the bad jokes.

All right, without some of the bad jokes. But once we get into it, you'll see it's not exotic at all. Whether you face some hard cases holed up in a bank or just have to talk your wife out of another weekend at Mom's, you can work it out. You can get what you want and not blow up anyone in the process.

Seriously. Even if you've never thought about negotiation before, a lot of this will start to sound familiar. I call it "applied common sense"—taking what we all know to the next level. Because we're always negotiating, every day of our lives.

Which brings me to one last point: Always be a Boy Scout. *Always be prepared.*

Myself, I'm not a Boy Scout, but I do love their motto. You just never know when you're going to find yourself negotiating with your life—and maybe a lot of other lives—on the line.

This hit home for me—literally—one night on a bridge. My partner and I responded to a call of a jumper up on the tower. When we got the call, it was still light, but with traffic and contingencies, by the time we started up the sun had set.

Let me tell you this about bridge towers—they are higher than high, and the ladder rungs seem to move away from you while you're climbing. It takes a long time to go up. By the time we were about a hundred feet up that evening, we were in total darkness.

Neither my partner nor I had brought a flashlight. Even a little key chain light would have been helpful. We climbed another two hundred feet or so in total darkness, skinning knuckles and bumping our heads on the side of the ladder. God must've been smiling on us, because somehow we made it to the top, and in this case talking the jumper down went fairly smoothly. But it could easily have turned out differently; one of those bumps could have turned into a disastrous slip.

So now I keep a pocket flashlight on my key chain.

And one in the glove compartment. And another under the seat. And another in the trunk.

Of both cars.

Hey, there's no such thing as too prepared.

CHAPTER 1

FIFTY NINJA WARRIORS AT YOUR BACK

Teamwork and the different roles in a negotiation.

I started out in the hostage rescue business as a ninja, one of the guys with the fancy black suits and the high-powered rifle. Following a police career that began with walking a beat, I trained as a sniper and became part of the New York Police Department's 9 Truck emergency service unit. Most days, I felt one very small step removed from being a superhero. Nothing, I mean nothing, was too big for me to handle. I believed—hey, I KNEW—I could solve any problem.

One day I responded to a building where a drug dealer was holding a group of other drug dealers hostage. Now I have to admit, the fact that the other hostages were drug dealers themselves—well, let's say that gave the situation a certain slant, and it was definitely something I thought about as I set up my shooting rest across the courtyard from the apartment where they were being held.

But things were put into slightly different perspective when I found out something else—the drug dealers had a four-year-old daughter, and she was being held hostage with them.

I went from superhero to impotent bystander in about three seconds, because I could see that no matter what any of the members of our unit did, saving that little girl with our high-powered rifles would be nearly impossible. The apartment was dark, there were only a few windows, the lines of sight were bad, night was falling. If the gunman decided to kill that kid, her only hope was God, not us.

I got down, put my Steyr on the rest, and took my position. I asked my shooting partner, Tony Sanpiatero, "What kind of a weapon does he have?"

Tony answered, "He says he has a machine gun but he's full of shit."

As I began squinting into the scope, a barrage of .45 caliber slugs exploded from the apartment across the way. The hostage taker had a World War II–era "grease gun"—a primitive but deadly hand-held machine gun—and emptied at least half the clip at the building where my partner and I were sitting. Glass flew everywhere, dust, dirt, you name it. About the only thing the gunman didn't hit was us.

Somehow, I managed to stay calm and look down my scope. All I could see was the muzzle flash, a blinking yellow and red flame at the left corner of the window. My finger tensed on the trigger.

Shooting would have been the worst thing in the world I'd ever done, because I didn't really have a target. I couldn't 100 percent guarantee a hit. Sure, I could have fired at the flash and probably nailed it. But that might or might not have gotten the bad guy. And *probably*'s not good enough when you're working 9 Truck.

In little more time than it takes to blink an eye, the firing stopped. Fortunately, the bad guy hadn't hit anyone.

"Well, I guess he's not lying," I told my partner. "He sure as shit does have a machine gun."

You have to have a pretty dark sense of humor to be a city cop. You laugh to get rid of the tension sometimes, and that was one of them.

Unfortunately, it was about the only laugh we had for the next several hours as the impossible situation dragged on. The hostage negotiators made contact and started talking to the bad guy. Finally, the commander told us the situation had stabilized. No shots had been fired for a while; there seemed to be no imminent danger.

He was doing more than keeping our spirits up. At that point our rules of engagement changed. We no longer had a green light to fire.

And of course, the gunman came dead in my scope maybe three minutes later.

How tempted was I? A squeeze of the trigger and the whole thing would be over.

I thought about the little girl. Here was my chance to save her. Part of me, a large, large part of me, wanted to squeeze the trigger. I could visualize it easily. The bullet would nail the SOB dead between the eyes. He'd fall back on the floor. The girl would be free.

I'd be a hero.

Except, to shoot I'd have to disobey orders. I untensed my finger and just watched as the hostage taker moved out of sight.

Time dragged. Finally, roughly twenty-five hours after the situation began, we got word that the bad guy was coming out. The girl, the other drug dealers, and the bad guy came out of the apartment. The crisis was over.

One other person remained inside—a woman who'd been hiding there from the very start. She'd ducked under a bed and kept quiet the whole time.

The bed was right behind where I would have shot the hostage taker when I had him in my sights.

Would she have been hit by my bullet if I'd fired? If the shot went through his body clean, would it have nailed her too?

I honestly don't know. Thank God it's one of those things we *never* will know.

What I do know is that everyone in the apartment got out without any injuries. They were saved not by a ninja, not me, but by a hostage negotiator—a mouth warrior. Another member of the response team had used words, not bullets, to save five people. He was the hero today, a true hero in every sense of the word.

Until that point, I hadn't really considered how important the negotiators were. I hadn't even thought of them as being part of the team. My view of the world was through a high-powered scope. It was a powerful view, but a limited one.

Make no mistake: If we hadn't had our guns trained on him, no way the bad guy would have given up. But from that day on, I realized how important negotiators were. I had a different view of the team concept of handling difficult situations. And I was very glad I hadn't blown everything by disregarding the rules that underlay the team approach and taking my shot.

The rules had been drawn because the commanders had stood back at the start and realized the goal in that situation wasn't to plug the guy; the goal was to get everyone out alive. To meet that goal, everyone had to do his or her job. Even if that meant not shooting when the suspect was in their sights.

A TEAM FIRST

A lot of people are on the line when police departments deal with hostage situations. You can break this large team down into three basic groups:

- Negotiators.

- Technical people who set up communications and that sort of thing.

- Tactical people, which includes the snipers and others you see pouring out of SWAT vans on TV. That's 9 Truck, in NYPD parlance.

The number of people in each group depends partly on the department and partly on the situation. Obviously, a big department will generally have more resources and therefore more people on the team. At NYPD, dozens and dozens of police officers can be involved, even in what we might consider a "routine" crisis. And in a big crisis—fuhgetaboutit.

In "real" life, the technical aspects of negotiations are usually taken care of. You want to talk to someone, you pick up the telephone. And even though you may think it's the right thing to do, you can't call in a SWAT team when your daughter asks if you'll pay for her hotel room after the prom. So with a nod to the techies and the guys with the body armor, we'll focus on the negotiating team.

THE THREE JOBS IN NEGOTIATING

The ideal hostage negotiation team consists of five people: the commander, the primary negotiator, the backup or coach negotiator, the scribe, and the floater. Each has his or her own role to play during negotiations. The primary negotiator negotiates. The backup/coach offers suggestions and moves in when the first negotiator needs a break. The scribe keeps track of what's going on. The commander makes the decisions. The floater runs errands. (We call him a floater because "gofer" doesn't sound glamorous enough, though that's what he is—hey, somebody's got to run for the pizza.)

Each person on the team corresponds to a different task common to all negotiations. Each task is different, requiring a different set of skills and even a different "head" or mind-set. Most of us can do without pizza, and even large departments must sometimes forgo the luxury of having a backup negotiator nearby, but the other three jobs represent critical functions in any successful negotiation. Even if one person is handling all three roles, he or she must be aware that these critical jobs are all different:

• Negotiate

• Keep track of what is going on

• Decide

All of these jobs are equally important. All come into play during every negotiation—even the one you'll have tonight with your spouse over what television show to watch. Even if you're a one-man negotiating team—especially if you're a one-man negotiating team—it pays to remember that concluding a successful negotiation requires three different activities.

Which brings us to a key truth about negotiations:

Roles must be clearly defined and considered before negotiating.

Which usually translates as:

The negotiator is NOT the decision maker.
The decision maker is NOT the negotiator.
Out of my kitchen, you crazy fool.

If you have a civics class bent, you can think of it as a separation of powers. It's critical in hostage negotiation, and it'll work for you every day as well.

A lot of people understand that the roles of the scribe, say, and the negotiator are different. But they get hung up on the separation between the negotiator and the commander. They figure if they're in charge, they should be the one running their mouth. It can be a real ego thing, worse than me and my superhero hang-up.

Separation is critical to ensure objectivity in decision making. And it can also be a useful tactic. Separating the final decision maker—call him (or her) "the boss"—from the negotiator gives the negotiator one more tool to work with. You can use it to build rapport with the other side: You and I are working on this problem together, then we'll deal with the boss. You can use the commander as the bad guy:

"Gee, you know, if it were up to me, I'd wheel that getaway car right up to the door for you, fill the tank with gasoline and stuff the trunk with hundred dollar bills, but the boss, he won't go for it. . . ."

Or to give a more familiar example:

"I really want to pay through the nose for that car, but the wife . . ."

But the separation of roles isn't just a tactical thing. It keeps the negotiator from making a bad decision, or a bad deal.

There is a tendency during some negotiations—even with bad guys—to get into a situation where you want to please the other side. You actually start liking the person. That can make you lose sight of your goals in the negotiations. Having to refer to someone else counteracts this.

ONE-MAN TEAMS

For a lot of business and personal negotiations—say with your kid over bedtime—negotiation is a one-man or -woman gig. A single woman buying a house on her own can't and shouldn't rent a husband just to negotiate the deal. But it's the concept of separation that's important here, not the game card. Negotiating and decision making can be separated in a multitude of ways, not just by using physically different people. A one-man team simply has to adopt strategies to make sure the roles stay separate.

These strategies are not rocket science. You can go with the ol' "Let me sleep on it" tactic, which lets you step away from the table and change roles. "Sounds like we're almost there," you tell the other person. "But let me just take a day to think it over."

A slight variation is the time-honored "Let me discuss it with my spouse/partner/parakeet" line, used even when the spouse/partner/parakeet is the last person in the world actually making a real decision.

Let me sleep on it. . . .

I have another appointment but I think we're almost there. . . .

You get the picture.

MERGING THE ROLES

So, what if the other side tries to break down the separation?

The easy answer is: Don't let them. And if you understand how it's commonly done, you won't.

There are only two tactics the other side can use to get the negotiator to merge the roles. To be fair, they may not see it as an adversarial tactic at all;

from their point of view they're trying to close the deal. They think the negotiation is done, whereas you know that the negotiation isn't done—you're not ready for the closing—until the commander reviews the negotiated terms.

One tactic a negotiator can try when someone asks for more time to make a decision is the "ego play." The other is the negotiating deadline.

The ego play works as some sort of variation on the old line: "Who wears the pants in your family, anyway?"

Sure, generally it's done much more subtly, but you get the idea. The best way to deal with ego plays is to recognize that that's what's going down. We all need a stroke now and again—but don't look for it from the other negotiator.

I'll go into deadlines in greater detail in Chapter 8, "The Two Ds— Demands and Deadlines." Along with demands, it's one of the two Ds that rookie negotiators fear but old pro's love. You can skip ahead, or you can remember this until we get there: Most deadlines are bullshit.

And most of the ones that aren't can be negotiated.

And the ones that can't are bullshit.

If the deal you've negotiated isn't strong enough to allow you a few hours of contemplation or whatever you need, it's not a good deal. Period.

SEPARATION, SEPARATION, SEPARATION

As an NYPD negotiator I had absolutely no problem remembering that I wasn't the commander: He was generally the guy in the room with the shiniest badge and the largest hat size. In most everyday situations, you can keep the roles separate by planning for them to be separate before negotiations begin.

Plan to negotiate, plan to break when you've got your best possible deal—when you've nailed down all of the difficult issues. Plan it right down to the exact words you want to use. If you're negotiating on the telephone— a favorite in hostage negotiations, since it's a heck of a lot safer than standing ten feet away from a guy with a gun—write it at the top of your notepad. Hey, tattoo it to your wrist if you have to. There are worse things on people's arms, believe me.

COMMANDER SETS THE GOAL

But the commander's role is not just reviewing the negotiations after the framework of the deal is worked out. On the contrary. The commander has to set the goal for the negotiation *before* the negotiation begins. If I want to buy a new car, for example, I know before going into the showroom how much I'm willing to pay. The "boss" has already authorized intelligence gathering, processed the information, and set a reasonable goal before handing that goal over to the negotiator.

It works the same way in hostage negotiations. The commander often makes the important decisions in a negotiation beforehand. At a minimum, he or she lays out the parameters for the negotiations and a possible deal.

Let's say I'm talking someone down from a bridge, for example. Well, the bosses make it pretty obvious what they want before I climb the million-foot ladder to the top to start working: Get the person down without him or her getting hurt. So when I'm about to close the deal with the jumper by getting him or her to step down, I'm not going to say "Hold it, let me climb back down the ladder and make sure it's okay for you to give yourself up peacefully."

We got *after* covered, we got *before* covered, that just leaves us the middle, right? So what's the commander doing during negotiations?

He or she is making sure the other members of the team are functioning together. The negotiator has to keep receiving relevant intelligence as he negotiates. For example, if the earth has suddenly shifted so the jumper will only fall two feet if he lets go of the window, the negotiator has to know about it. And ditto if the manufacturer is now offering a $10,000 rebate on the chariot du jour.

Repeat after me: "The negotiator is not the decision maker. The negotiator is not the decision maker. The negotiator is not . . ."

GETTING IT DOWN

Probably the most overlooked job on a negotiating team is the scribe's. Let's face it, the negotiator and the boss get all the glory; the scribe's just a dude with a pen. But the scribe's role is nearly as important as the others', and in "real" life negotiations provides an important record to check the final agreement against.

A hostage situation can go on for several hours or even days; a few have lasted weeks or more. Negotiators spend a lot of that time talking, and even more listening. Even the best listener is going to forget what someone said ten hours before. A scribe acts like a combination secretary and historian, keeping track of anything significant.

A one-man negotiator can keep track of developments by taking notes as things proceed. Too often, though, the notes are overlooked in the heat of battle. Just as a hostage negotiating team must plan to make use of all its members, an individual must build in time to review his or her notes along the way.

A friend of mine recently completed a long series of negotiations for a contract to purchase property. The negotiations, which involved a lawyer type as well as my buddy, stretched over a period of weeks. They reached some broad agreements quickly, but with the legal beagle involved, there was some rather complicated work on contract provisions. Part of the negotiating was done by e-mail, which, along with various notes, provided a good record of what transpired.

Except that—you guessed it—the lawyer neglected to review all the e-mails and ended with a deal memo that skipped a critical point. Luckily, he had copied my friend on the e-mails. In his role as commander of the team, my buddy gave the negotiator a hot blast where it would do the most good, and the lawyer went back to work.

Had there been no record, it's very possible they would have missed the point entirely, resulting in a great disadvantage to the buyers of the property. At best, they might have caught it at a later stage and had to reopen the negotiations. That might have cost several weeks of further delay as the point was bantered back and forth.

REASONABLE GOALS

Reasonable goals are important in any negotiation, and it's the commander's job to set them. But that begs the question: When was the last time you worked for a reasonable boss?

Hey, no comment. I got my pension to think about.

Seriously, while there are always exceptions, even the best negotiator is going to have to rely more on luck than on skills to reach an unreasonable goal.

You can't set a reasonable goal unless you know what you want. The more specific you are about your wants before you go into the negotiations, the better you'll do in the end. Think of it this way: If your goal is just to get the guy off the bridge . . . well, let's not go there.

Setting the specific goal is part of knowing the territory; you can't do it unless you've scouted out the area and done your homework. If you haven't, then you aren't in a position to negotiate—and position is everything, as we'll discuss in the next chapter. But let me just beat the reasonable boss thing to death. It's important in a negotiation to be realistic beforehand as you set your goals. If you're trying to buy a new house, it makes no sense to think you're going to negotiate the price down to a hundredth of the asking price.

Some people try and use unreasonableness as a negotiating tactic. Personally, I've never found that a very powerful tool. It immediately establishes that the other side is the only pro in the room, putting the negotiating team on uneven grounds. Worse, it's pretty easy to deflect from the other side. (We'll also talk about that in Chapter 7, "Is He a Psycho, or Just a Maniac?") But look, if it works for you, that's cool. Just remember there's a difference between whacked-out as a tactic and whacked-out as a goal. Use any tactic you want, but keep your goal realistic or you won't achieve it.

SUMMING UP

Easy stuff, right?

There are three basic jobs on a negotiating team, ideally handled by three different people: negotiator, scribe, and commander.

One-man teams should build in ways to separate the roles.

Start by thinking about the roles differently.

Adopt strategies to separate the different processes as much as practical.

CHAPTER 2

POSITION IS EVERYTHING

Before you negotiate,
be mentally and physically
in the right place.

Snipers arriving on a scene always try to establish a position where they have a good line of sight into the crisis area. This isn't rocket science: You can't hit something you can't see. The trick is finding that ideal place without exposing yourself to overwhelming danger.

Negotiators do the same thing. A good negotiator chooses the best spot to negotiate from.

You're thinking, Hey, Dominick, you made a metaphor. Wow, what a poet.

Yeah, I'm a regular Henry Wadsworth Longfellow.

I do mean it metaphorically; we should always negotiate from a metaphoric position of strength. That happens not only if we do all our homework beforehand, but if we know every possible argument the other side will use, have an answer to every question it will raise, and have a solution that is so win-win even George Steinbrenner couldn't turn it down. Negotiators should always go into a session holding all the cards . . . just as guys should always remember their wedding anniversary and Valentine's Day.

Whether that's possible or not I leave to your own experience.

I mean *position* literally. Where you stand, how you sit, and like that.

You have to be comfortable to negotiate. Physical and mental comfort as you negotiate is vastly underrated as a strategy. A hostage negotiator needs to have a place where he or she is secure from attack and has a means of communicating with the hostage taker as well as the scene commander. Nearly as important, the negotiator needs to be in a place comfortable to operate in—which means simple things like being able to sit in a decent chair or not having to go too far when nature calls.

He or she also has to be in a good mental position to negotiate. Hostage negotiations are very intense forms of negotiation; they take immense concentration under huge stress. That's why our ideal teams have someone to handle the dreck work that comes up. It's also why a coach and backup negotiator is always alongside to keep your energy and ego up when they sag.

Most negotiations aren't life and death. Still, you have to be able to concentrate. For most of us, that starts with being relatively comfortable. That's commonsense stuff. Don't try to negotiate the purchase of a new house the day after your father's funeral. Wear clothes that make you comfortable—but not something that's going to make you feel inferior. And don't wear tight new shoes when you enter the boss's office to ask for a raise.

A LONG-TERM HEAD

One of the important things police negotiators learn is to go into every negotiation as if it will be a long-term event. Having that attitude right at the beginning of the process helps set up a successful negotiation. And if you think you're going to be at it for a while—if you're taking the negotiation seriously, as all negotiations should be taken—then you're going to start by making sure you're physically comfortable and mentally ready to work.

Dumb example time: Few years back, a negotiating team responded to a domestic-type dispute in a suburban neighborhood. It turned out that a man had barricaded himself in a house for some trivial reason and was refusing to come out. No weapons had been observed, and in fact there seemed to be some question among the police officers responding to the scene whether the man was really barricading himself in there at all.

"This is bullshit," said the negotiator. "I can deal with this easily."

It was an early fall afternoon in the Northeast, one of those gorgeous 70 degree days just before the leaves start changing colors. The negotiator figured he'd have the guy out in a few minutes and get back in time to knock off early for dinner.

Except that the person in the house turned out to be pretty serious about not coming out. And he turned out to have a weapon no one had known about.

The afternoon turned into the evening, and the evening to nighttime. The temperature dropped to 50 degrees, then dipped to 45. The negotiator, still in shirtsleeves, froze his body parts off. By the time the man inside the house finally agreed to come out, the negotiators were suffering from hypothermia and the commander looked like one of those ice sculptures you find at fancy weddings.

I'm kidding about the hypothermia, but it *was* damn cold.

You're not in a position to negotiate unless you're comfortable, and unless you're prepared. Don't start negotiating until you're ready.

THE PHONE AND OTHER TOOLS

As a general rule, hostage negotiators use a telephone to do their job. It's the preferred method of communication with a guy with a gun for obvious reasons; or to put it another way, face-to-face BS'ing with an armed psychopath is vastly overrated. As a general negotiating tool, I think the phone is fantastic. Most Americans are pretty comfortable with it, and it offers certain advantages when you're dealing with difficult points. For one thing, the other side can't see the notes that your coach negotiator is shoving in your face—or if you're a one-man negotiator, the notes outlining your research and the flow you want the discussion to take. And unless you have a telephone with a video setup, they can't study the emotional reactions on your face, which for most people tend to be harder to control.

Of course, that also means you can't use the power of personal, immediate contact. A disembodied voice on a telephone can remain just that—a disembodied voice. If you're looking to establish rapport early on in a negotiation, or maybe jump-start a situation that's gotten a little static, a face-to-face may help move things along. Just make sure the other guy doesn't have a gun.

E-mail and instant messaging are other technologies in the negotiator's toolbox, and I think we'll be seeing them used more and more in the future. In many ways these are similar to the telephone, though even more limiting in communicating emotion—at least in theory.

ENEMY TERRITORY

Ah, the boss's office—enemy territory. A lot of people think that any negotiator on unfamiliar ground is at a disadvantage. And not just because the boss purposely limits seating to straight-back metal chairs. According to "negotiation as war" thinking, the person who establishes the negotiation setting will be the ultimate winner of the negotiations. Small victories in preliminary skirmishes add up.

From my point of view, that's all wrong. First of all, I don't buy the premise that someone inevitably "loses" a negotiation. A good negotiation, even in a hostage situation, arrives at a solution that everyone can live with—literally. And I don't like the "negotiation as war" thing at all; if I did, I'd still be a ninja, trying to blow people away.

In my view, negotiations are the opposite of war. And if it's important for you to be comfortable, then it's important for the other guy to be comfortable too. Which means, if I'm asking for a raise, I *want* to do it in the boss's office. Honest. He'll be comfortable there, even powerful, and that's what I want—I want to persuade him to use the power he has to get me the raise.

Newspaper reporters tell me they'd much rather interview a subject in his or her own home than in their newspaper office. The familiar settings put people at ease, lowers their guard. The same thing is true in negotiations. Comfortable people tend to be much more reasonable, or at least less distracted, which helps negotiations proceed. The more secure the guy across the table is, the easier it's going to be for him to focus on the meat of the negotiation, the stuff that you're trying to get. If he's uncomfortable, if he feels threatened, then that's what the negotiation is going to be about.

One more point about dress and comfort before we move on. While it's important to feel comfortable yourself, you don't want the person you're negotiating with to be uncomfortable. That means leaving the jogging suit you haven't washed in a month at home when you're going to a fancy law office to hammer out a divorce agreement. A barrel, on the other hand . . .

American business culture has gotten very casual over the past decade or so, but clothes can still be used to send subliminal messages and set a tone. I'm not telling you how to dress—no laughing out loud, please—but I am telling you to be aware of the message your clothes are sending. The message is often subtle and complex.

Suit and tie in the car dealership? Guy's got money, a businessman . . . maybe too much money, maybe a little stuffy, tough to negotiate with once he draws a line in the sand . . . not a lot of time, in a hurry, wants the bottom line.

T-shirt under a business suit at a lunch? Creative type, casual . . . might not pay attention to details . . . confident . . . full of himself, arrogant, thinks he's a star. . . .

Very short skirt—well, you get the idea. You have to be aware that you send messages in all different ways. Don't send messages that are counterproductive. Send messages that fit with your personal style and comfort level.

Some negotiators spend a lot of time psyching out their opposing number's preferences, and dress accordingly, usually to show that they're a member of the same club, sometimes to cause the opposite reaction, kind of the "shock and awe" theory of negotiating. The idea is to use the other guy's reaction to their advantage. It works for them, but it seems to me that can easily go way too far—I'm not wearing high heels and makeup to any negotiating session, thank you very much.

Other negotiators say that because it's impossible to completely control another's perceptions, they try for a fairly neutral appearance, preferring to come off bland rather than skewing the situations. I think that's a safe bet. Personally, I prefer to err on the nicely packaged but casual side, aware that I'm sending exactly that kind of message—easygoing guy, not particularly threatening, the sort you can talk to in a bar. Depending on the situation, I might wear comfortable jeans, a sport shirt, sport jacket, easy on the jewelry. A watch is an important tool in negotiations—"got to get running" is always an instant out—and I prefer an old-fashioned clock dial and a nice band: not a Rolex, but just nice enough to hint that I've done okay in life, or at least at the racetrack last week.

You're not me and you shouldn't try to be. Fit your clothes to your personal style, then fiddle with it for the negotiation.

THE BUSINESS LUNCH

Have you ever tried to use alcohol to grease the skids in a negotiation?

No?

Then you must not have been a guy out on a date.

But I digress.

Lunch—and dinner and breakfast and cocktail parties and baseball games and yadda-yadda-yadda—have become accepted, even expected, settings for business negotiations. Breaking bread together is a good way to establish a working relationship where negotiations can take place. Maybe this is just my Italian-American heritage talking— *"Mangia!"*—but food and the whole idea of sharing a meal together puts everybody in a relaxed situation. We're all human together.

Now look, there is such a thing as being *too* human. Lunches are a zillion distractions just waiting to happen, like the steak that was supposed to be rare getting delivered well done. Some people are going to find it too distracting to do any real negotiating, though they can use it successfully to build rapport. For me, casual, friendly settings can put both sides at ease and add the human element that builds rapport. And rapport helps a negotiator do his job.

ALCOHOL?

No lectures; I'm not your mom. Personally, I see nothing wrong with a beer or whatever over lunch while you're negotiating. Just keep it at an appropriate level. Alcohol definitely dulls the senses.

And, uh, if you're not feeling well: Don't negotiate.

Ought to be obvious, but . . .

HOSTILE TERRITORY

So what do you do if you're forced to negotiate in hostile territory? Traffic's blaring at you and people are screaming, "Jump! Jump!"

Well, at the NYPD, we would try to control the scene as much as possible in pretty obvious ways, setting up barriers, moving people back, etc. The idea was to dilute the chaos as much as possible, and that strategy carries over to any negotiation. The trick is to remember that you're creating a *mental* place as much as a physical one.

What you want to do is shift from the casual chaotic place to a focused, negotiating, business place. By initiating the shift, you can set the agenda briefly, which allows you to focus on what you think is important.

You're at lunch, you've been chatting in a casual way about the details of a contract. This is your only real opportunity to discuss them and get them nailed down. How do you shift the space?

One way would be to take out a small notebook and say something along the lines of, "Okay, let's just nail down these two or three points. . . ." Your tone of voice—and the paper and pen—have immediately created a place where the negotiations can continue. You've just set up a police line around the block and pushed everyone back.

The risk here is that your opposite number may not be prepared to negotiate or get serious. That's not optimum, but it's not a real setback. Because her hemming and hawing tells you that the casual talk that led to this point was just that—a scouting mission on her part prior to the real thing.

(Come on, guys, use some common sense: If you take out a pad and a pencil on a date, I don't want to know you. It was just an example, for cryin' out loud.)

Salesmen shift the mental space all the time as they prepare to close a deal. They have all sorts of tricks and shortcuts—car salesman takes out a bid sheet or whatever they're calling them these days and starts putting numbers down; appliance guy in Sears starts talking about payment terms. Now the thing to remember when you're on the other side is this: That shift is not the END of negotiation; it's the START. You've just mentally walked from the bar to the table at the back of the restaurant. You are in a different place—but that place is not the finish line.

MENTAL COMFORT: BEING PREPARED

No matter where you negotiate, no matter which pair of loafers you're wearing or what color your blouse is, you have to be in a mental position to negotiate.

Let's say your roof leaks when it rains. Before you pick up the telephone and call a contractor, you have to know exactly what it is you want. Now, if you know a lot about roofs—or if you see a three-foot-wide hole—that's pretty obvious. You can draw up a simple plan: Call three companies, get three estimates, choose the best. But if the problem is more complex—you can't see where the water's coming from, or you think maybe this might be a time to build the addition as well as fix the roof— you may have to take several preliminary steps before the actual negotiations begin. These are jobs for the other members of the team—the intelligence person, and then the commander. The negotiator doesn't get involved until they have scoped the situation and a solid goal has been set.

Leaky roofs are easy to deal with, in a way—it's pretty clear there that you're not going to start haggling on price before you actually know what's going on. But let's go back to my buddy with his complicated property deal. He knew from experience that the overall money paid would be the major focus of negotiations; there'd also be a lot of hassle over exactly when and how it was paid. But he also knew that details in the contract language could be nearly as important, covering the various contingencies and approvals involved in the purchase. One was particularly tricky: Who would pay for the engineering work needed for zoning approval, which the whole deal was contingent on? Most often the buyer does, but in this case my buddy was willing to pick up some but not all of the cost, even if he bought the property.

So he decided to work his negotiations in two stages. Stage one involved the price; that was the main focus of talks, which went off and on for a few weeks. Then, with the parameters of the deal set, the team essentially took a break from negotiations. A proposed contract was drawn by the other side, following the usual procedures. Only when my friend and his lawyer had the contract in hand did they begin the second round of negotiations. They'd used the time off to gather information about the effect the engineering work would have on adjacent parcels the seller owned and how much it would cost to have the work done for just those pieces of property.

The decision to break the negotiations in two wasn't simply tactical. My friend wanted to be prepared to fine-tune the agreement, but knew that wouldn't be possible until he had an estimate of how much the other party would benefit. It also helped to have the exact language in front of him. He avoided a lot of wasted energy, and maybe even a potential deal-blowing dispute, by waiting until he was properly positioned to negotiate those points. He was able to focus the second stage of the negotiations and achieve exactly what he wanted without getting sidetracked by other elements of the deal.

Which brings us to the rule of position:

Make sure you're in position to negotiate before you start negotiating.

This may sound simplistic—man, I *hope* it sounds simplistic by now—but you can't start negotiating if you don't know what you want. If you're not sure whether you want the ranch house on Cherry Street or the Cape Cod on Meadow Avenue, you're in no position to start talking. Unfortunately, many of us start negotiating before we really have a goal set out. Is it the Camry or the Accord you're after? Until you're sure, you're in no position to negotiate.

This is especially important when you're negotiating what might be euphemistically called "domestic situations." If you've ever talked with a teenager about what time they should be home, you know what I mean. The more explicit you are about what you want—home before midnight, no excuses—the better the odds of getting what you want.

Though we are talking teenagers here.

EVERY JOURNEY BEGINS WITH A MAP

Knowing what you want gives you a goal to shoot for. Getting there, of course, is most of the fun.

Getting there involves tactics and strategy; we'll spend the rest of the book discussing them. But part of being in position to negotiate—maybe even the most important part—is having that map in hand before you open your mouth. Or to put it slightly more eloquently:

Make sure you have a plan for the overall negotiation process before beginning.

That means the negotiator—and the tactics are his call—should know not only his goal and what's negotiable and what's not, but the order he wants to proceed in before he starts. We'll open with a casual lunch, mention two important points, then break. Two days later, a session with all the serious issues. Another casual meeting if necessary, heart-to-heart talk, get the outlines of the deal to the commander and close.

Bing-bang-boom, you're married before you know what hit you.

GETTING IT DONE

Basic stuff, right? Hey, it's all basic stuff—the problem is getting it done.

One September morning back in 1992, I was sitting in traffic in Queens on the way to work, thinking about how great the weather was and how quiet it had been in the city over the past few days. Bad combination—good weather, quiet times; sure enough, my beeper went off.

The number in the screen belonged to the chief of detectives. One thing I knew before I managed to pull out of traffic and reach a pay phone: He wasn't calling to ask me to pick up doughnuts on the way in.

Two idiots with guns had decided this would be a fine day to rob a Chase Manhattan bank in Brooklyn, and when things got snarled up, they'd barricaded the doors and taken hostages. Maybe they rented *Dog Day Afternoon* the night before—could be, since the botched robbery that led to the hostage situation portrayed in the movie took place maybe half a mile from the bank they had entered while I was driving in to work. Just like in the movie, things went sour.

Al Pacino was nowhere to be seen when I pulled up. But the chief of detectives and ten or fifteen other high-ranking bosses were.

"Hey Talk-to-Me, come over here," said the chief.

Talk-to-Me was one of my nicknames at the time. It was a good one, certainly preferable to others that cannot be reprinted here.

"Listen to this and tell me what you think," the chief said, taking me aside and laying out the basic situation. The would-be bank robbers had asked for a van. They wanted to put the hostages inside and drive ten blocks to a police station. At that point, they promised to release the hostages.

Several of the chief's underlings were telling him to go for it. Obviously, they were after his job.

"What do you think?" asked the chief.

Well, I couldn't tell the chief precisely what I thought, because there were so many expletives involved and he had a shinier badge than I did. But I did make my basic opinion clear. You don't take a situation that is basically contained and un-contain it. You don't subject hostages to danger unnecessarily. You absolutely don't give the bad guys a means of escape.

And if you're a chief who's in any way comfortable with your job, you don't take a shot at giving the dozen or so news crews on the nearby rooftops a chance to do a live version of *Disaster at High Noon*.

"Something goes wrong and the subjects try to make a run for it, you have a major shoot-out with three hostages right in the middle of it," I pointed out as diplomatically as I could. "The whole incident will be televised live throughout the nation. Who's going to be blamed?"

The chief turned pale. He turned and walked back to his so-called advisors. "We are not going to let them drive themselves anywhere," he said in about as firm a voice as I've ever heard.

Now let me point out that the chief—and his advisors—were all pretty intelligent guys. To be the head of detectives in New York City you have to have a range of skills that goes well beyond being a good detective. I couldn't do it. I don't want to do it. And even though I love to make fun of them, most of the people giving the chief advice were pretty sharp too. But even in the best force with the top people working together, bad decisions can be made.

What happened—or I should say *almost* happened—was something I call in my classes "the quick fix syndrome." We're going to go into it in a lot of detail in the next chapter, but the thing to realize now is that things are not always as good or as easy as they sound. There is no such thing as a quick fix. Not to pick on them—well, okay, I am picking on them—but in my business, and possibly in yours, quick fixes come when supervisors who have not been trained in the art of hostage negotiation get involved without really understanding the big picture.

Fortunately, the chief was smart enough to trust the system he and others had set up beforehand. They let the negotiators do their job. Ultimately, he had faith in the system and the people he put on the team to carry it out.

You have to have faith in the team and in yourself if you're going to succeed as a negotiator. Trust the process, even if the negotiation doesn't seem to be making headway. I'm not saying you can't review your goal and positions to make sure they're realistic. Many times that's necessary. But losing faith in your process and your team is a guaranteed way to fail.

Success doesn't mean that you get everything you want 100 percent of the time. That's not success—that's perfection, and perfect you and I ain't. Not every negotiation will reach its goal.

Let me repeat: You ain't going to get what you want every time you negotiate; that's why you need the guys with the guns, or Plan B. Plan B does not equal failure; it is the alternative.

A successful outcome that meets your goals is possible in most situations you'll encounter. So if you don't get it this time, relax, trust yourself, and move on.

SUMMING UP

It's important to be comfortable when you negotiate—important for you, critical for your opposite number.

Pay attention to hidden messages you may project before the negotiations start, especially with your clothes and jewelry.

Realize that the surroundings and tools you use—a fancy restaurant, the telephone—can subtly influence the tone and shape of the negotiations. Be aware of it, and use it to your advantage as you build rapport.

Don't negotiate until you're ready to negotiate, which means:

- Know what you want

- Have a map for getting there

CHAPTER 3

DON'T GIVE
THE BAD GUY A GUN

Before you begin to negotiate, know what you will not give up.

Ever hear the joke about the hostage negotiator who gave the guy he was negotiating with a loaded gun?

Neither have I. Because that is no joke.

START RIGHT, FINISH RIGHT

In hostage negotiation, the bad guy's weapon is usually pretty obvious—he's got a gun, or a bomb, or some sort of weapon that he exploits as he presents his demands. The negotiator has to arm himself as well, not with a physical weapon—that's the ninja's job—but with intelligence about the situation and the person he's negotiating with. He goes into the negotiation with a clear goal: Get the people involved out alive. He also has a simple guideline that applies to every hostage situation, though how it plays out can vary: Don't make the situation worse. Before negotiations begin, the responding police agencies and the other members of the negotiating team take three key steps that will help the negotiator shape what happens:

- *Conduct initial intelligence.* How many bad guys are there? How many people are in the bank with them? What are the exits in and out? How'd they get here? (That usually tells you how they hope to leave.) All of this information is provided to the negotiator when he arrives so he knows the situation before he starts talking.

For negotiations involving purchases, initial intelligence is the most important step.

- *The commander decides the specific goal, and ultimately decides what is negotiable and what's not.* Getting the good guys out alive is the goal of every hostage negotiation. But that goal is counterbalanced by other things, most obviously the need not to endanger other people. So even that very obvious goal has to be adjusted and amended. It is not an absolute rule in hostage situations that the ninjas will go in if the bad guys start shooting. Granted, Plan B is often put into effect. But the department regulations never tie the commander's hands; every situation is different.

  For everyday negotiations, deciding what you're willing to compromise on can be the most difficult part of the process. Ideally it's done before the negotiation, but the process of negotiations may bring you back to this step again and again. That's another reason it's important for the negotiator and commander to be separated.

- *Set your negotiating parameters: Know your "out" and your "push."* Once the decision has been made on a goal and the parameters of a possible deal, the negotiator does his own planning, coming up with a basic road map on how to meet the goal. The "out" is the alternative, the Plan B, the ninjas in the hallway. If this deal doesn't happen, what does?

  The "push" is simply the approach the negotiator is planning to take, the way he adapts his personal style to the negotiation. How hard is he going to push? Which buttons? This can't be dictated, since it's a matter of personal style. Someone who is not comfortable with direct physical confrontation may still be a decent negotiator if she can take that into account as she conducts the negotiation. The phone is a great equalizer—someone who's six-eight sounds pretty much the way someone who's five-two does. Being resolute about goals and positions is important; shouting and screaming about them is not. As a matter of fact, it's almost always counterproductive.

INITIAL INTELLIGENCE

Hostage teams that have worked together for a while develop their own rhythm for gathering intelligence. Ideally, a separate person will be assigned not only to gather the basic information about the situation, but to update it as the negotiation goes on. Intelligence includes information both on the situation itself—the physical layout, were shots fired, etc.—and things that may help you deal with the other person: Is he married? Where does he work? Who has influence over him? And so on.

Everyday negotiations can take advantage of the same pattern. Remember that this stage involves looking at *your* needs before examining the possibilities of filling them. Most negotiations in everyday life are more open-ended than hostage situations—there may be many houses you could live in, or many refrigerators you can buy. Knowing what you need allows you to narrow down the choices to a specific few. That's good—but you're not ready to negotiate yet, just to do more research.

Let's say you're in the market for a new automobile. There are literally hundreds of models to choose from, each one of which will get you somewhere. You examine your own needs and decide that they come down to commuting to work locally and hauling wood and other items to renovate your house on the weekends. That helps you narrow your goal to a pickup truck. Your next move is to gather information about pickup truck possibilities, which leads you to conclude that you want one of the so-called compact pickups, which offer relatively decent gas mileage while still being able to handle a few bags of cement and an occasional two-by-four. You find there are four possibilities that will be relatively easy to research. That's a good number—not too many to research, but more than enough possibilities to give you some flexibility as you go.

At this point you're not ready to negotiate, but to gather more detailed information. This includes not just finding out the invoice and sticker prices, but things like options and possible colors and extras and how hard that stinkin' CD player is to work while you're driving sixty-five and drinking coffee and talking on the cell phone. Generally that means going to the dealer and kicking tires, if not a salesman. It's only after all of the kicking gets done—all of the intelligence is gathered—that the commander makes a decision, picks one truck as his goal and another as Plan B and hands off to the negotiator.

The number one problem people make in sales situations is to begin negotiating when they're still gathering information. They haven't even decided what they want, and they're talking seriously about money and service warranties.

There are reasons for this. Number one, the salesman is making a photocopy of your license and talking about how his mother needs one more operation to survive. And admittedly, human nature is going to push you at this stage to want to jump in and get it over with. Don't do it—you're the intelligence guy, the researcher, the gal with the thick glasses spending hours on the computer. Negotiation doesn't begin until you've gathered all the information. Then the commander takes over.

WHAT'S NEGOTIABLE AND WHAT'S NOT

Before beginning any hostage negotiation, negotiators are trained to take a piece of paper and draw a line down the center. On the right side are things that are negotiable; on the left are things that are not. The list starts out with the obvious and gets more subtle.

For a hostage negotiator, the goal is to get the suspect to surrender with dignity without the loss of life. Negotiable items would generally include things like allowing food and water into the scene. Non-negotiable items would include things like alcohol, which could make the negotiations considerably more difficult to conclude. The lists tend to be similar from negotiation to negotiation, though there are always some new wrinkles popping up.

In everyday negotiations it's at this point that the commander decides what he or she really truly wants, and what he or she is willing to give on. Unless you've done your initial intelligence gathering, you're not going to be able to draw up your list of negotiable and non-negotiable items. Without it, you're not ready to begin. To go back to our pickup truck example, you may decide that four-wheel drive is a critical feature because of the weather where you live and the fact that the vehicle has to get you to work through rain, sleet, and snow. You may also decide that while nice, a CD changer is not essential.

Ideally, the intelligence gathering shows you the cost or value the other side will place on each item. This is obvious in a car deal, where each option has a stated price. It's not quite so clear-cut in most other business situations, however. In most situations, including hostage negotiating, intelligence gathering continues throughout the negotiations. New information comes in; assumptions are checked and rechecked.

Again, the commander makes the call on what the goal is, not the negotiator. It's important, even in the face of new intelligence, to keep the roles separated.

WHAT'S YOUR OUT?

With a goal and the general parameters of a possible deal worked out, one more important decision has to be made before the negotiator can step up to the plate: What is the alternative to the deal? What if the negotiations fail? What will happen? What's your "out," the alternative to a negotiated settlement?

Hostage negotiators know the alternative if they can't get a deal. The ninjas go in, the plane blows up, people die. It's not pretty.

It's also not a failure. It's Plan B. Sometimes negotiations don't work, no matter what you do.

It's horrific, but that's the way it is. You have to accept it. If you can't live with Plan B, there is no Plan B.

And you *always* have a Plan B.

You need an alternative. You need an out. Without a viable alternative, you have no basis for negotiation.

Fortunately, most negotiations don't involve dire situations. Knowing what you will do if you "lose" the negotiation or simply walk away is critical. If your boss doesn't buy your arguments for a raise, will you look for another job? Will you try again in a few months? Will you bring bag lunches to work for the next year?

Knowing your out does a couple of things. For one thing, it helps set realistic goals in a negotiation. But just as important, it can be psychologically reassuring during the process. Because even if the consequences are very dire—people dying is about as dire as you can get—by seeing the possible result, you know that failure of the negotiations is not going to mean the end of the world. That helps you project confidence during the negotiations that's not a phony front. You know which door you're taking if you walk away from the deal. And knowing that gives you power as you negotiate. Worst-case scenario: I'm going to XYZ Company and get a better paying job.

THE PUSH

Now that you know exactly what you want, what's negotiable and what's not, and what the alternative is, it's time to draw up a plan. You want to know *how* you're going to push.

While your exact style is going to differ depending on your personality, there's a general shape that every negotiation follows: establish rapport, get information, work on the deal. At this point, you want to think how and where you're going to do this.

In a hostage situation, the negotiator will start by trying to put the subject at ease and build up a rapport. More than likely the rest of the team is still gathering intelligence, and the negotiator is helping this phase along, taking stock of the subject's personality.

The negotiator's first goal is to lay the groundwork for the rest of the negotiation. He'll listen actively—a concept we'll touch on down the road—and solicit information that will be helpful in shaping the rest of the negotiations.

At this stage he may avoid mentioning hostages, deadlines, anything that doesn't contribute to the building up of the rapport. (And as a matter of fact, he never calls them hostages; instead he may ask how many people are inside, emphasizing that these are human beings, not things or bargaining chips.) He won't go into the specifics of his position—won't say what's negotiable and non-negotiable. The focus should be on the hostage taker and establishing rapport.

For this to work, the negotiator has to be—or at a minimum appear to be—nonjudgmental. He doesn't approve of what the subject has done, but he is respectful of the other person and is interested in his or her emotions. In a hostage situation, the subject may ventilate a bit, and the negotiator listens. To use the pop psychology lingo, the negotiator may validate the emotions so he can move onto more logical problem solving as the session continues.

I can't tell you how important it is to let the subject ventilate during a hostage situation. It gives the negotiator all sorts of important information. A subject venting talks not only about the problem, but often what we can do to resolve it. We listen, we learn, we respond.

Same thing in an everyday negotiation. Granted, the person on the other side of the table probably won't be ranting about what's important. But he or she will tell you what they want—and if they don't, encourage them to do so.

On a five-man negotiating team, the backup/coach negotiator monitors this process, helping the primary negotiator stay away from trigger words that may provoke a bad emotional reaction, while at the same time picking up on key things the subject says that reveal information about his state of mind and his demands. On a one-man team, of course, this has to be done by the negotiator himself, and that's why having an outline of the direction of the negotiation before talks begin can be very useful.

THE SPLIT-PAGE METHOD

One of the little tricks I like for remembering what's important is to simply take a piece of paper, draw a line down the middle, and on the left side of the top write NEGOTIABLE, and on the right side write NON-NEGOTIABLE. You can fill in as necessary, based on your initial intelligence. If it's a car, you might put something like: DVD player with headrest screens, CD changer, GPS navigation system, extended warranty, maybe even the color of the vehicle. Under NON-NEGOTIABLE go your limits, like the model vehicle you have your heart set on, an absolute cap of $25,200—dream on, right?

Of course, after the commander reviews the list and reviews certain inalienable facts about kids and long car rides, you slide the DVD player and headrest screens off the negotiable side and place it on the non-negotiable side, but you get the idea.

It's not exactly high-tech; I don't think a sheet of paper costs more than a nickel even in New York, and I doubt you'd plunk down a couple of hundred dollars to attend a seminar where that was the only piece of advice.

But I have to tell you, it's saved many a negotiation. The simple rules are sometimes the very best rules, and this simple one works for everything from hostage negotiation to buying a car or refrigerator.

BASIC PRINCIPLES

Three rules are important at any stage in a negotiation:

- Never lie.

- If you make a promise, keep the promise.

- If you don't ask, the answer is ALWAYS "No."

QUICK FIXES

The first principle, "Never Lie," ought to be obvious. This is as much practical as moral. Lies are counterproductive because they hurt the trust you're trying to establish during the negotiation. You have to assume that eventually the person is going to be able to find out the real information; if that happens and they realize you've lied, at best it demolishes the rapport you've established. At worst, the other party may use it as a legitimate reason to end negotiations altogether.

The thing about lies is that they are always tempting. They're seductive. They're almost impossible to resist sometimes, because you know, you just know, that if you say them you'll get what you want.

Usually not, but boy it seems that way at the time. A lie is a quick fix to a complicated situation—and that's exactly why they're dangerous.

We had a hostage situation in New York City once where I was negotiating over a speakerphone so the rest of the team could hear what was going on. I forget all of the nitty-gritty, but basically there was a fellow with a gun inside an apartment. We talk on the phone for a while, a long while, and finally we get to the point where he says, "Look, I'll put down my gun and come out, but you have to promise me you're not going to handcuff me."

One of the department chiefs—the NYPD has several—was standing across from me at the time. I happened to look up and saw that he was nodding his head. Then he mouthed the words, "No handcuffs."

Now I have to tell you that there is no way in the world—*no way*—that a person in that situation is not going to be handcuffed. It's a matter of safety. The guy has just held a few dozen officers at bay with a gun. If he's not restrained, what will prevent him from making a grab for a weapon once he's outside?

The chief knew that, and the chief fully intended that the man be handcuffed. But the chief figured that by claiming he wouldn't, we'd get the guy out, have the hostages safe, and be done with a very dangerous situation.

But telling the suspect that he wouldn't be cuffed was a lie. I wouldn't do it. I asked him to repeat what he wanted. The chief started waving his hands in my face—I mean, I was getting a full-blown dramatic presentation here.

"I have a situation here," I told the subject. "Let me put you on hold and get right back to you."

As soon as I hit the button, the chief was all over me. Now at that point I knew most of the chiefs in the department, but this guy and I hadn't worked together before. Which I guess made me a little more polite, at least at first.

"What's up, Chief?" I asked.

"Tell the guy okay."

"I'm not telling him that. He's got to be handcuffed."

"Tell him."

"I'm not going to do it."

"I order you to do it."

"You're ordering me to do it?" I said.

He nodded.

Well, an order is an order. I picked up the phone and told the subject, "Look, you're going to be cuffed. And you're going to be cuffed behind your back. That's the way it is. That's our policy. I can't change that."

"Okay, Dom," he replied. "Now I know I can trust you. I've been arrested before. I know how it goes. I just wanted to see if you were full of shit or not."

A few minutes later the guy put the weapon down and came out.

Of course, the chief and I had a little personal time in the hallway as the handcuffed suspect was taken away. He wanted to know why I had disobeyed a direct order.

"Are we talking chief to detective, or you to me?" I asked.

"You to me," said the chief.

"Well, you didn't know what you were doing," I explained. "You saw a quick fix and thought that would solve everything. In this business, there is no quick fix. When something looks like one, that's exactly the time to stick to your guns."

I had an advantage over the chief, not just because of my training, but because I had been dealing with the guy for a while on the phone and had the entire context: I somehow knew he was testing me. But the incident emphasized for me that there is never a quick fix, and that you have to stick to your basic principles or you'll be tripped up in the end.

PROMISES

Promises are an important tool in hostage negotiation, helping the negotiator establish rapport and credibility. I promise to do something for you,

you see that I do it, you realize I have credibility. We have a relationship—I promise, you promise.

Generally, promises start small and work toward the big one—the promise to surrender. A hostage negotiator will often go first, making a small promise he knows he can keep. One typical promise a hostage negotiator might make would be to tell the subject the truth. Small promise, but an important one. Down the line, maybe food and water would be delivered in exchange for a number of hostages. As promises are made and kept, the negotiator gains credibility—he (or she) can deliver on his promises.

The corollary to this is to never make a promise you can't keep. You don't promise that the suspect won't be cuffed when you know he will be. It's a quick fix that will bite you in the end.

Negotiators should remember that there are really two types of promises—explicit promises and unspoken ones. The explicit promises are pretty obvious: I promise to send food in, you promise to send out three hostages. But there are unspoken promises as well. And it's important to keep them.

They begin with the agreement to start negotiations at a certain time and place. Saying that you'll get information about a certain item is an important commitment—a promise, whether it's stated that way or not.

Keeping promises does more than demonstrate to the other side that the negotiator is consistent and trustworthy. It shows that the negotiating team has the power to follow through on an agreement. It's also a chance to build up trust with the person on the other side of the negotiation. Coming through on a promise is like pushing down on a seesaw—I helped you up, now you do the same for me.

SAY WHAT?

Being macho means never asking for directions. Ever. For some reason, it's like an admission not just of ignorance, but of impotence. As someone who travels a lot, I know the feeling very well. Just asking a question like "Where's the restroom?" for some reason makes many guys feel like George

Custer when Chief Sitting Bull and his five thousand Sioux warriors came up the hill.

On the other hand, it's better than the alternative.

Some negotiators believe that asking questions is a sign of weakness. On the contrary, I think it's a sign of strength. The most powerful question you can ask the other person is: *What do you want?*

Think about it.

If the negotiator can ask it, then he's implying that he can fulfill that need. That takes power.

Now I may not, and I may not want to, fulfill all the needs of the other side. That's not what the definition of a win-win solution is. But by asking, I've clarified the situation greatly. I've gotten the other side to tell me his or her main issues in the negotiations that will follow. If nothing else, we won't spend a lot of time trying to figure out what those issues are.

Asking what exactly the other side wants can be especially important when dealing with complicated legal matters. Looking at a clause in a contract recently, one of my associates was baffled by the legalese. The clause seemed to take away all of the associate's rights—and yet maybe not. The lawyers couldn't figure it out either. Finally the negotiator went back to the other side and asked simply, "What are you trying to say here?"

The other side thought about it, then struck the clause.

Talk about your easy solutions . . .

CONCEPT 51

I'm not a mathematician so don't get on my case, but I have a kind of a mathematical theory that involves numbers and percentages that I call "Concept 51." This is the goal all negotiators strive to achieve when they're dealing with a hostage: trust.

I think of trust as a scale that runs from zero to 100. Zero is mistrust, no trust, the position where you would put the marker if you didn't believe a word someone said, even if they were looking at a calendar and telling you the day. In hostage negotiations, the police are starting their negotiations with a hostage taker from a position of mistrust. Zero. Null. Nada.

Let's face it, the people we deal with have not had too many good experiences with the police. I cannot remember the last time I invited a hostage taker to Thanksgiving dinner. We have to take that situation of no trust and move it up the scale pretty fast. We're not aiming at 100; that's unrealistic. We want to get to a point on the scale where trust is greater than mistrust: 51 percent.

Sometimes we can calm a subject down pretty fast and build trust that way. We lay out a solution, a way out with dignity—not there yet, but we're moving. Maybe we're at 35 percent. The subject asks me a question and I answer truthfully; we go for a bit, we get to 45 percent. I start working on ensuring the subject that he will not be hurt when he comes out. He states that he believes me and wants to come out but has to think about it.

We've reached 50 percent.

Getting that last little bit of trust in this situation, the last climb, may be the hardest part. Now, we don't have to go very far—just 1 percent. But like a baseball team that's struggled to get over .500, the big gains have all been achieved; from here on out we're looking for small, incremental things to build trust.

I think it helps as the rapport builds in an everyday negotiation to remember that it's tough work getting from 50 to 51. Rapport is critical—but it's not the end of the deal.

POLITENESS AND RESPECT

How do you address a potential mass murderer?

You call him "Mister" until he tells you that you can use his first name. And you do it politely, and with all the respect that another human being deserves.

I know, I know—you're thinking I'm out of my mind on this one. You call potential mass murderers "Sir?"

But I do. I have. I admit it can be very hard. I have a real hard time dealing with child abusers and lowlifes like that. Call it a personal prejudice, I guess. But knowing that, I work at it and try to be even more professional in that situation—more polite, more nonjudgmental. Because when I'm doing the negotiation, I'm not dealing with the slime bag—I'm dealing with the human being. And all human beings deserve respect. Show a person respect and in most cases they'll return it.

I mentioned earlier that lying is an absolute no-go thing for me. The thing I've found is that once you lay that idea out, people respond to it. On one of my very first negotiations, it turned out that the subject who'd taken a hostage and barricaded himself inside an apartment had grown up on the streets in the Bronx. Looking to establish some sort of rapport, I told him I grew up on the streets too. Different neighborhood, but basically the same sort of place. And then pretty much by accident I said, "Do you want me to lie to you or tell you the truth?"

Well duh, he wanted the truth. Which is what I was going to give him anyway. The thing is—and I hit on this by accident—by asking him that, I showed him I wanted to treat him with respect, no BS. The question is now one I ask all the time to get to the first yes. I talk specifically about that strategy in Chapter 6, "The First Yes," but for now, remember how a simple, everyday question can help you build rapport and establish the trust you need to proceed.

SUMMING UP

Don't give the bad guy a gun—know what's negotiable and what's not negotiable before you start.

Conduct intelligence gathering before starting to negotiate. Continue gathering intelligence as you negotiate.

The first goal of the negotiator once negotiations start is to establish rapport.

There are no quick fixes in negotiations—don't trust one even if it looks like a gimme.

The best way to build rapport with someone is by showing them respect. Don't bully them, don't look down on them.

CHAPTER 4

CONTAIN,
NEGOTIATE,
CLOSE

There are three phases to every negotiation. Finish one before you go on to the next.

Hostage situations can be broken down into three phases. Phase one is containment—the first goal of the police forces responding to a crisis is to contain the situation. If bank robbers have taken over a building, at a minimum you want to keep them in that building. If they have ten hostages, you don't want to give them eleven. If they have three guns with a dozen clips of ammunition, you're not going to send in a fresh case of shells.

The time up until containment—and until the subjects realize and accept that they're contained—is probably the most volatile. The bad guys have guns or knives or bombs or whatever, they're pumping gallons of adrenaline through their veins, and by definition they're not thinking straight. I don't know anyone who keeps precise statistics on this sort of thing, but it's common knowledge in the law enforcement community that the most dangerous time of a hostage situation is during the initial takeover. That's when weapons are most likely to be used.

The uncertainty about what is going to happen during this time puts everyone at danger. My goal during this stage is to put everyone at ease. When I say everyone, I mean everyone, starting with the hostage taker, hostages, negotiators, SWAT personnel, and our commanders. Everyone is experiencing an adrenaline rush. The hostage taker is trapped and feeling a fight or flight decision. The hostages may be trying to figure out if they should fight or try to escape. The SWAT team members have raced to the scene at 100 mph. The commanders are faced with the enormous responsibility for the lives at stake.

Just the simple tactic of getting the hostage taker to talk and allow a little time to pass has the effect of calming everyone down. We're not really negotiating in this stage—we're calming down and getting ready to negotiate.

Phase two involves the negotiation itself. The negotiating team makes contact and begins to work with the subjects. The negotiator will work to establish a rapport on a very simple level, asking for a name, treating the subject with respect. This stage does not begin until the situation is contained. There's a practical reason for that—the subject really has no reason to negotiate, or even talk to you, until it's clear that his options are limited. Containment leads to negotiation: I'd say in most crisis situations, the fact that a tactical squad has responded to the scene and cut off the possibilities of easy escape makes the subject want to negotiate. He's looking for a way out. That doesn't necessarily make him cooperative: Hey, the guy's got a gun, remember? But it does give him an incentive to start negotiating.

Hostage negotiators know that they have a great advantage. Something like 98 percent of all the hostage takers and barricaded people you deal with want to live. That tells the negotiator right from the start that a deal can be worked out; all he has to do is come up with one that everyone can live with, literally. But this is true in most everyday negotiations as well. The car salesman and the real estate agent want to make a sale. The company shopping for a new retirement management program wants the service. All you have to do is find a deal everyone can live with.

The last phase of the situation comes in the surrender—closing the deal the negotiator has worked out. This is also a very dangerous time. We've all heard of buyer's regret; imagine how it plays out when the buyer has a gun. Hostage negotiators will strive to have no surprises at the closing, and part of the negotiations will involve working out exactly how the people surrendering should move and behave.

THE BASIC MAP

It's important for the negotiating team—whether one man or five—to understand these different phases, because different things can happen in them. You don't have a basis for negotiating unless you have containment. To put it another way, if you don't know which house you're going to buy, you can't negotiate with the seller. There's no basis for anything but a casual discussion, *not* a negotiation. Even the discussion is likely to be all over the place. Likewise, you can't close a deal until you've put everything in place—until the negotiations are finished.

The negotiation stage can stretch on for quite a while. Some are done in different stages. And some of the stages use different negotiators.

Take publishing, for example, an area I hadn't known until I started working on this book. (And no, I didn't negotiate the deal myself; that's the agent's job. I got to be the commander.) Negotiations generally take place in two very different stages. In the first stage, which is generally considered the most difficult, the general terms of the deal are worked out. This involves broad issues like the amount of the advance or the up-front money for the author, a royalty rate, the places where the book can be published, and similar issues. But after the parties come to an agreement, there's a second stage involving the specifics of the arrangement. A contract must be worked out. And believe me, the hassles over the legal language can get very involved. There's no deal until all of these issues are squared away.

A common mistake made by negotiators in phased negotiations like this is to think that since the first stage is generally the most important and contentious, the second stage isn't even a negotiation. Wrong, wrong, wrong. All stages of a negotiation are equally important—even if the issues being discussed are less immediate or even lower on the priority list of wants. They still contribute to the goal. The negotiator still has a serious job to do.

Take a labor contract, for example, where the negotiators have agreed in principle to a three-year contract with a raise of 3 percent each year.

They set the overall parameters and then announce that they have a deal.

But it turns out that they don't, not yet. Because the contract language hasn't been worked out. Disputes can easily arise at this second stage: Was it 3 percent over the base? Or 3 percent over the previous year?

Now in that example, the issue should have been worked out in the first phase. But I can't tell you how many negotiations ultimately founder—and how many bad deals actually get signed—after similar details are overlooked. In the rush for an agreement—which both sides want—important details are often overlooked. When they are, realize that you are still in the negotiation stage.

SMOOTH IT AIN'T

Of course, it's easy to plot out how things *should* go: First responders get to the scene, discover there's one man in a building, remove people nearby from harm's way, get the building isolated, set up barricades, prepare a nice pot of coffee for the negotiators. . . .

But real life is usually pretty messy. There have been times when a crisis situation that was thought to be contained suddenly wasn't. This routinely happened during the 1970s and early 1980s with airplane hijackings, when the aircraft would be refueled and allowed to leave an airport, sometimes without even any concessions from the hijackers. I'll spare you my tirade, but it is important to admit that things often don't go according to script. Hostage negotiators sometimes find themselves back at square one after hours and hours of work, and you may too. That's why one of the most important qualities a negotiator can have is *patience.*

The NYPD Hostage Negotiator checklist emphasizes that time is on the side of the negotiators. One of the basic goals of the checklist and its related procedures is to slow down the incident. This helps the negotiating team think. It makes it possible to gather more information. It also helps cool emotions.

Taking your time and being patient help negate the real-life messy factor. Stepping back from the process can give you an opportunity to put the messiness in perspective. Sometimes if you strip away the emotional response, you realize that you are still on your game plan.

BREAKING CONTAINMENT

They may not call it that, but everyday negotiators need containment before they can start negotiating. If you're buying a house or a car, you contain your negotiations to that specific house or car, and to a general range of features and prices. By the way, that doesn't mean that you've given up your out. Your out is not part of the negotiation. It's an alternative. I'm not sending the ninjas away; they're the reason the folks in the bank want to negotiate in the first place.

So what do you do when someone breaks containment—for whatever reason they completely change the parameters of the deal?

The most important thing is to take a step back and examine where you are. Remember that the process has started over again. You haven't wasted your time; you've invested in the overall deal. But you do have to reassess where you are.

An old sales strategy called "bait and switch" uses breaking containment as a tool. The strategy is pretty obvious: The new set of tires are advertised as being fifty bucks apiece; you get to the showroom, and low and behold, the last of those tires went out the door five minutes ago. But the salesman has another set for $250. . . .

That specific practice is outlawed in most places these days, and even where it's not, few salesman actually interested in making a sale will try it, since the reaction of many customers will be instant anger. But there are much more subtle variations. For example, the advertised price may not include installation or, in the case of those tires, balancing, which will add ten or twenty bucks a pop to each tire. One of my favorites is the rebate ploy, where the cell phone is advertised as costing $100 after the rebate.

Assuming you fill the form out right. And good luck finding it.

Think about it this way: Breaking containment happens anytime you think you're negotiating about x and it turns out that the other side wants to talk about $x + y$. Or just y.

The best strategy for dealing with obvious bait and switches is probably just to walk away. But hostage negotiators don't have a choice about the sorts of situations they get called to. And many times in a business negotiation, y comes up more or less on its own.

As long as you realize the process has to start over—which means new intelligence, new command decision on goals, new negotiations—you'll be all right.

TURNING IT AROUND

From a negotiator's point of view, it often doesn't pay to worry too much about the motives for another person's tactics. What may seem almost evil may be a product of poor team dynamics or lousy decision making. That isn't to say that someone with a gun isn't out to kill you; it's just that you should make judgments about someone's moral fiber and its relevance to the negotiations very warily.

Look, if you do think someone's out to screw you, go to the ninja's right away—Plan B is always in order. It's just that more often than not, the other guy really isn't out to screw you at all.

Let's turn the old bait and switch around for a second. A customer comes into a Chevy dealership and says he wants to buy a Malibu. Salesman starts working out the deal, gets a good price down, and then all of a sudden the customer says, "Gee, I'd like an Impala instead."

Ploy? Change of heart?

Does it matter? The salesman has already learned a lot about the customer, certainly more than if the customer had just walked in. The customer is saying that he wants a deal—just not the one they've been talking about.

The salesman should take a step back and ask the customer to clarify what he wants, realizing that he's not yet at the point where he can negotiate. Once the customer's needs are established—once the intelligence is done—he can get back to the negotiating stage and have a real leg up, since he's already built a rapport.

TRUST

Before you can get down to the serious issues of a negotiation, you have to have some sort of relationship with the person you're talking to. Some guys do this with small talk; others will lay out their understanding of the situation, starting with the least controversial matters and then going logically, or as logically as possible, to the more difficult areas.

For me, the best way to start is to ask the other side what's important to them, and let them drive the discussion agenda, at least at first. In my experience, you're not really going to be able to negotiate until you have some sort of relationship in place. Asking the other person what's going on builds the rapport and also tells you what they value. By the time you're ready to start talking about important points, you already know what they are.

In a sales situation, rapport is sometimes built during the containment stage prior to negotiation. Let's say you're a salesman in a stereo store and a customer comes to you with a general interest in buying a stereo. She's not very specific, and so you don't really know what you're going to negotiate on. Rather than charging off to sell her the latest model from XYZ Corporation, you can start to build trust by asking her what her needs are. How often does she listen to music, is she going to watch DVDs in the same place, and on and on. Yes, you're striving for containment. But by showing an interest in her needs—not *yours*—you're setting the stage for negotiations.

FLOW AND TIME-OUT

Once the sides are exchanging positions, negotiations are in full swing. Important points will be raised, sometimes as demands, other times with less threatening words that will add up to the same thing. The flow of the process can vary greatly depending on what you're negotiating. There are no hard and fast rules for how this ought to proceed.

As we'll see in Chapter 8, "The Two Ds: Demands and Deadlines," some negotiators like to get the tough stuff out of the way first, while others will tend to push it off. Personally, I like to work with a few easier issues first, building trust up, then tackle the more difficult issues, with a few easier points held in reserve. That's because the easier points can be used to keep negotiations moving in the right direction if they bog down on serious disagreements.

In a perfect world, your intelligence gatherer has figured out what the sticking points are going to be before you sit down to negotiate. This of course gives you plenty of time to contemplate a strategy for dealing with these points. Well, guess what? The world ain't perfect. Sticking points tend to be sticking points precisely because nobody thought they were going to be problems ahead of time. Difficult issues are, in the final analysis, difficult issues.

Hostage negotiations tend to be pretty intense, and sooner or later they come down to one sticking point—the suspect has to surrender. With all the attention on that one issue, it's important for the negotiator to be able to ease the tension at times. Sometimes when the pace of the negotiation bogs down, the hostage negotiator will just stop talking about that point. He or she will change the subject to something else: kids, baseball, the price of paint in Poughkeepsie. It's like taking a time-out. Human beings need to relax every so often.

Real time-outs are also part of the negotiator's tool kit. Simply breaking for a few minutes—or days, in an everyday negotiation—can do wonders for the process as a whole.

CLOSING

The second most dangerous time in a hostage negotiation is the very end, after an agreement has been reached and the subject comes out to fulfill his end of the deal by surrendering. The guy comes out through the doorway. He's nervous, and the guys in the tactical squad are nervous too. The hostages are nervous, I'm nervous, everybody's nervous. Somebody sneezes, and all that nervous energy suddenly gets put to very bad use.

The surrender is basically the close of the deal, the time our "customer" signs on the bottom line. The key to getting him or her to sign is to make sure there are no surprises.

Hostage negotiators always work out the surrender terms and the procedures as clearly as possible before concluding the deal. We aim for no surprises at the end. That should be the goal of everyday negotiators as well. What are *all* the terms—not just the important ones, *all* the terms. The negotiation is not complete until they are specified.

I hope this comes under the heading of very, very obvious, but let me say it anyway: It helps to put the terms of a complicated deal in writing. Write the agreement down. I'm not talking about a contract, though obviously that's an important part of many business deals. I mean, simply, write it down. Heck, you put your shopping list on paper, don't you? Or is that why you're out of toothpaste and there are twelve quarts of milk in your fridge?

Seeing things on paper or, these days, on a computer helps objectify the issues. The scribe on the negotiating team should always write down the other side's terms, not just because something important may be forgotten, but because it helps keep the negotiations on an objective level. If the points are something you can see on a piece of paper, you're less likely to get too emotionally attached to any one of them.

Of course, if your scribe's handwriting is as bad as mine, you may not be able to decipher them at all. But that's another story.

LAST-MINUTE GRABS

One of my friends was recently negotiating to do a job for a contractor. It wasn't a particularly difficult assignment, and the general parameters of the agreement were known in advance. He agreed with the contractor to do the work for the same fee he had been paid in the past, pending the work-out of the language.

And then, after the arduous prospect, the other side suddenly decided that my friend should be paid $100 less than he had on the other job.

I'm not kidding. The contract was for several thousand dollars; it had taken weeks to work out the deal, and in fact the contractor actually needed to have the work done pretty quickly. The contractor had actually intended on negotiating over a smaller sum, but had made a mistake during the preliminary stages of the negotiation. Of course, the contractor didn't admit that there had been a mistake; he just presented it as a take it or leave it.

Now to be honest, my friend would have settled for less money than the agreed figure during the negotiations because there was slightly less work involved in the job. What angered him was the fact that the change was made at the last minute, after the deal was set. He interpreted the sudden price reduction as a macho game by the contractor.

Weighing everything, my friend decided to go ahead with the contract. But guess what? He was so mad that he relegated the work to one of his assistants, giving it decidedly less of his own attention than he ordinarily would have. The job was done, but to lesser standards than it would have had the last-minute switch not occurred. And a long business relationship ended.

Was a relationship that had worked well and profitably for many years worth $100? Was the fact that the assistant took a few days longer to put up all the drywall—this was a house—and maybe missed in a few places, more important in the big picture than a hundred bucks?

I guess only the person who ended up not buying the house after a second walk-through could say for sure.

BUYER'S REGRET AND OTHER TRUST BREAKERS

Some people feel that a person who attempts to change a deal at the closing, after it's been negotiated, is untrustworthy. Since trust is the basis of negotiations, according to that line of thinking, there is no room to deal with them again in the future.

My view on that depends on the situation. It is true that some people are just playing games and looking for whatever advantage they can have. But in most instances, last minute snafus like that arise because the negotiators haven't covered all of the bases during the negotiation. Terms must be as specific as possible, or there simply isn't a deal.

What about buyer's (or seller's) regret?

Last-minute hesitation is a natural emotion, and you see it most often in things like house sales, where the object being sold is more than just an object. When ten years of your life have been put into a place, the issue isn't so much the price, but simply the fact that you're leaving those memories behind. On the other side of the transaction, a first-time buyer who's never enjoyed the pleasures of a heavy mortgage and outrageous property taxes is bound to start feeling nervous even if she's calculated her payments a million times.

Establishing trust early on in the negotiations allows the person on the other side to ask directly about these regrets or fears and to address them sympathetically, without coming off as a phony. The words may differ according to the negotiation and your style, but the message you're trying to send is simply this: "I understand your emotions, and they're natural. I'm nervous too."

It's hard to be on the receiving side of a last-minute switch. The key is to step back and see the terms in their overall context. Was $100 that much compared to the overall contract? Probably not.

Unfortunately, stepping back from the situation at the closing can be extremely difficult, because that's precisely when your emotions are involved.

EMOTIONAL VULNERABILITY

Both sides are vulnerable at the closing. They've already emotionally attached themselves to the deal. In the case of my friend, he'd already decided how he was going to spend the money. He didn't have to go through with it, of course, but his position would have been that much better if he hadn't started eyeing that television set before the deal closed.

I think it was a television set. Maybe it was a new drill. Whatever. The point is, you do not have a deal until the closing. Don't start acting as if you do.

The negotiating team should lay out the understanding carefully before the closing. Reiterate important points: "You're going to have your hands up when you come out of the building." Don't take shortcuts: "We'll do what we did last time." Remember, there are *no* shortcuts in negotiations.

THE COMMANDER'S ROLE

In the first chapter I talked about the importance of having a full team in the negotiating process, or at least thinking of the different functions as separate. As the closing takes place, the commander must be the one to step back and review what's going on. At this stage, it often happens that the negotiator is too emotionally involved in the deal to make a judgment.

Friend of mine was buying a house a few years back that he knew would need a fair amount of work. He had his real estate agent negotiate a deal. She got a fair price within the parameters he had set, which in turn had been established with the help of a contractor. However, when the bank sent an assessor to look over the house and come up with a mortgage figure, the report came back about $15,000 lower than the agreed price.

What did the real estate agent do? Well, after saying that the assessor's report was wrong, she contacted the other agent and came back to my buddy with the suggestion that the agents would knock a few thousand dollars off their commissions to make the deal fly.

Every situation is different, and I don't want to make blanket statements about real estate agents and house prices and mortgage companies. But the real estate agent's reaction in this case told my friend that his negotiator was far too involved in the deal itself to stand back and make a logical conclusion about what to do. He thanked her and then, after analyzing the assessor's opinion, sent another house inspector through the building for a second look at the premises. The assessor's valuation was probably off a little, he decided, but not by that much. Armed with the new information, he had the agent go back to the buyer, with the bank's price as his goal. As it happened, the deal eventually fell through—and a good thing, my friend concluded, as not only had the agreed-upon price been a little high, but there was more work needed that hadn't been spotted during the original reviews.

WHERE'S THE NEGOTIATOR COMING FROM?

In that house deal, the real estate agent clearly was too focused on making the deal to use command judgment. Her decision was a quick fix on the situation, but it wasn't necessarily illogical from her point of view: A sale where she made a medium amount of money was better than no sale at all.

The commander, on the other hand, had to remember that his (and his wife's) goal was *not* to make a deal, but rather, to find a nice house that they could renovate at a reasonable cost. Their goal involved having a reasonable mortgage to make that happen; it also meant making sure the work would stay within a certain budget. Only by focusing on the goal rather than the deal was my friend able to handle the situation.

My friend decided to use the real estate agent as the negotiator in the next deal. He reasoned that he now knew a lot more about her negotiating style and how she would act in certain situations. I'm not sure I would agree with that—kind of a judgment thing, I guess—but he claims he gave her a much lower number on the next property and got a better deal because of it.

And, he says, he paid her full commission, even though her actions in the past showed he could have squeezed her there if push came to shove. Like I say, not everybody in the world is out to get you, not even in real estate.

SUMMING UP

Before you can start negotiating, you have to "contain" the situation.

In everyday negotiations, this means you have to know what you're negotiating about. You must know your goal before you can achieve it.

"Breaking containment"—switching the negotiating subject—is sometimes a deliberate strategy. When the other side employs it, recognize that you have moved back to the prenegotiating phase.

Closing the deal can be dangerous for the negotiating team. They become emotionally attached to making a deal once they've hit that stage.

CHAPTER 5

YOUR EARS
ARE YOUR MOST
IMPORTANT TOOL

Good negotiating comes down to good listening. If you can't hear, you can't negotiate.

So, the negotiating team has done all its homework. It knows what its goal is. It knows which areas it's willing to compromise on, and where it won't budge. It has a general map of the negotiating process.

Time to talk, right?

No. Time to shut up.

"TALK TO ME"

Working on the hostage negotiations squad at NYPD, I earned what has to be one of the most unique nicknames in the police field: "Talk to Me." It came from my habit of using that phrase during negotiations. "Talk to me," I'd tell the subject. "I'm listening."

Talk to me, not *listen to me*.

The hardest part of listening is stripping away the invisible filters in your brain that screw up what you hear. Those filters are worse than earwax. They distort what comes into the ear canal and send it unknowingly on to the brain.

We couldn't live without some filters. Filters let us sort voices from the car horns and jackhammers in the street; they let us recognize our kid's crying in a crowded room. Others are necessary for quick decisions—a fire alarm going off in the middle of the night is instantly recognized as a danger signal.

But during negotiations, our preconceived notions filter what we hear. If we begin a discussion thinking the deal will go a certain way, we tend to interpret the sounds around us according to those expectations.

On a five-man negotiating team, the coach or backup negotiator helps the primary negotiator get the wax out of his ears. He or she is a source of feedback and a check on what the negotiator is really hearing.

One-man negotiators can get feedback too. They just have to get it from the person they're dealing with.

Restate what the other side told you, to make sure you have it right. It's fine to be explicit about what you're doing: "I want to get this right" doesn't just tell the person on the other side of the table that you're listening; it's a sign that what he or she says is important—and by extension, that they're important.

EMPATHY, NOT SYMPATHY

Let's straighten one thing out right away. Hostage negotiators—all negotiators, for that matter—aren't aiming to sympathize with the person on the other side of the barricade. What they're shooting for is *empathy*: understanding the other person's emotions. The negotiator is not putting himself in the other person's shoes; he's figuring out where those shoes are.

In a hostage situation, understanding that a person is angry about, say, the fact that his wife wants to leave him, gives the hostage negotiation team a great deal of information and ways of influencing his behavior. Let's get obvious here for a second: If he's angry about his wife, you're not going to bring his wife to the scene. More subtly, if he's depressed, you may have to consider whether he'll try to commit suicide.

Everybody has emotions. Everybody has experiences. The two are not the same. Emotions are universal—we all know what sadness is like. Experiences are different. They are seldom shared. Negotiators shouldn't pretend that they have experiences they don't. They also shouldn't tell the person how they're feeling—that's a gimme for the response: "How dare you tell me what I'm feeling?"

What they can do is tell the subject how they sound to him. "You know, you sound pretty sad," is a lot different than saying "You're sad," because it's much harder to argue with. It gives the person on the other side of the barricades a chance to talk about what they're feeling (or not feeling) rather than arguing about it.

LISTENING FOR EMOTIONS

In a negotiation, a negotiator has to listen for several things at once:

- Verbal content

- Emotions

- Values

Every sentence that comes out of a person's mouth contains two different types of information. There's the verbal content: the literal meaning of the words. Then there's the emotional content: the meaning that comes from the way a person expresses it. A lot of times emotions tell you more than the words themselves.

Listening for the subject's emotions is very important in a hostage situation. For one thing, they can be a clue to their personality and mental state. But more important, listening to a person's emotions gives you a way to establish a rapport and to communicate with them. Without that basic rapport, there is no sound basis for emotions. In most cases in a hostage situation, a connection is established emotionally first.

Emotional communications are important in other negotiations as well. If you're negotiating a curfew with a teenager, believe me, 95 percent of what that communication is about is emotion; rely solely on verbal content and you're going to be grossly uninformed.

ACTIVE LISTENING

"Active listening" is kind of a buzz phrase in hostage negotiating. It's a reminder that listening isn't a passive activity.

When you're listening in a negotiation, you're trying to find out what the other side's position is. You're also listening for clues to what they think is important. Now in most negotiations, the person on the other side of the table is not going to give you a list of (a) everything he thinks is important, and (b) what he's willing to give up. On the contrary, he's probably going to try to disguise a bit of (a) and may not even know himself the details of (b).

I would counsel negotiators in most instances to give out as much of (a) as possible; get the important issues on the table where they can be dealt with and you can resolve them. But obviously you're going to hold back on (b), at least a little. And sometimes a negotiator doesn't know all of (a) until the other side comes back with (c).

When you're in listening mode, you can use your ears to determine (b), at least a little, from the verbal and emotional content he uses to describe (a).

Jeez, you'd think this was an algebra class with all these integers. What I mean is:

> *Usually, the way someone tells you about what he wants lets you know how much he really wants it.*

Even if the negotiator on the other side of the table is a pro and gets right to the outline of the deal—what's negotiable and what's not—you have to listen carefully to make sure the content and emotion match up.

MIRRORING AND VALUES

Reading back a person's emotions to them—telling them what we hear them expressing—is called "mirroring," and it's used by hostage negotiators to establish rapport with the subject. It can be used in everyday negotiations as well.

Now look, in most business negotiations, you're probably not going to be saying, "You sound a little sad." Not that there's anything wrong with doing that if the person really, truly, sounds very depressed—and you happen to have the phone number for the suicide prevention hotline on your cell phone. But realistically, that's not what we're talking about. The mirroring that goes on in most everyday negotiations involves the other side's needs and wants—which is another way of thinking about emotions. What are a person's values if not the things she or he feels strongly about?

Mirroring is an excellent way to clarify the needs and fine points in a negotiation. Mirroring also helps you gain more intelligence by refining your understanding of what's being said to you. Repeating what someone is telling you shows that you're listening.

But don't go crazy, guys—don't become the little echo that repeats everything the other person says that repeats everything the other person says that repeats everything the other person says . . .

Seriously, mirroring is a great way to keep the conversation and the negotiation moving forward.

GIVING YOURSELF AWAY

Some people are really lousy negotiators because they can't hide their emotions in situations where they think they can. Now in my opinion, just about anybody can negotiate anything—we do it all the time—but I'd be lying if I said that some people aren't better at it than others. Some people say more with their emotions than they think they are. The key for them as negotiators is pretty New Agey: They have to get in touch with their feelings.

Or at least what they're portraying as their feelings.

Friend of mine deals regularly with a business associate on contract matters. The associate doesn't realize—well, he may now, if he reads this book—but his voice has a very subtle quiver when he raises a point he's not sure of. That's not necessarily an indication that he's bluffing about the point itself, as my friend has learned. But it does mean that it's an area to be probed during their discussions. By keying on that quiver—and filing it away—my friend instantly knows more about his opposite number's position than the associate intends.

MAKE YOUR WEAKNESSES YOUR STRENGTHS

Let's turn that situation around a bit. Let's say you're the business associate and you know you get nervous when you're discussing certain issues. What should you do?

One strategy that would work to your advantage is simply to admit it's an important issue right up front. The idea is that you're not going to be able to BS the guy about it—and that shouldn't be part of your plan anyway, since you never lie. If you say, "Look, I'm a bit nervous talking money, but this is the figure I've been given to work with . . ." you've taken the focus off your emotions and put it where it belongs, on the money. Your emotion is not contradicting what your verbal content is; on the contrary, it's reinforcing it.

Of course, if we could always control and know our emotions, we probably wouldn't have any. But that's another subject.

MALICE IN YOUR HEART

Controlling people's emotions is always an area for discussion and disagreement when I give my hostage negotiation classes. I like to ask my students this question: "Can you control a person's emotions?" You'd be surprised at the answers I get. They range from a blunt "NO!" to "Maybe."

I follow up their answers with another question: "Has anyone in the class ever, with total malice in your heart, with total intent and dedication, set out to piss someone off?" The class usually laughs. Then I ask,

"When you set out to do this, have you ever not succeeded?" More laughs.

The point is, pissing people off is controlling their emotions. Our goal in negotiations is just the opposite: We want the person on the other side of the table to trust us, and even to feel good about themselves. I know it's not as much fun as pissing people off, but it's more useful for our goal. Use your talent to make people feel good about themselves and the deal.

SHUTTING UP WITH STYLE

Shutting up with style means you can't just shut up. You have to shut up in a way that gets other people talking to you. The more they talk, the more—usually—they reveal. You have to shut up in a way that gets people to tell you what you want to know.

Certain conversation "tricks"—I hate that word, but it's convenient—can keep a conversation going. You undoubtedly use several of them already, probably unconsciously.

First are the mirror phrases. You use these to signal that you're going to restate what the subject has told you, either to clarify it or to indicate that you understand it and are taking it seriously. Here are a few:

"So, is this what you mean?"
"Are you telling me . . .?"
"Are you saying . . .?"
"Let me see if I understand this . . ."

Notice how they tend to start with questions? The questions make the statements seem less threatening: Maybe I got this wrong, and here's a good chance for you to correct me.

Mirroring important points not only helps get them straight, it helps objectify them: If we're both saying it, it's something that exists outside us.

Out there we can work on it, fix it, put a little wax on it and get a nice shine to it.

Another technique to keep a conversation going is simply to be quiet for a while. Newspaper reporters and police investigators are taught that most people don't like a long pause or silence in a conversation. It's like the saying about nature and a vacuum—something has to rush in to fill it, even if it's only hot air.

And while we're on the subject of pauses, stopping mid-sentence while you're talking helps to emphasize that what follows is important. And for some reason I've never entirely figured out, it makes the other person think that you're actually trying to figure out what to say. Like it's important.

So . . .

You can use a pause. . . .

Even a sentence break—

To emphasize something. Even to seem . . . more intelligent.

Whether that's justified or not, I leave you to say.

MORE TECHNIQUES TO KEEP IT GOING

One of the simplest ways of asking for more information is to repeat the last word or words that a person said, but as a question.

"I was hoping we'd go on vacation this year," says your wife.

"Vacation this year?"

"Yes, to Paris."

"Paris?"

"It's so lovely in the spring. And with the money I just won from the lottery, our financial problems are over."

Yeah, right—in your dreams, Dominick.

But seriously, the technique works pretty well because it not only asks for more information, but it does so without narrowing down the direction that information can come from. The subject is volunteering what he or she thinks is important.

Open-ended questions—basically things that can't be answered yes or no—are the same way. They're requests for information, a bit more directed than simple mirroring or repeating, but still more liable to retrieve real intelligence than a sharply directed closed-end question.

That doesn't mean there isn't a time or place to ask yes or no. "Is this important to you?" is often an extremely valuable question. It's just not one you ask to keep the conversation going.

KNOW THYSELF: THE VOICE THING

Maybe it's my Italian-American heritage, maybe it's the fact that I grew up on the streets of New York, maybe it's something I picked up during my years as a cop and then a negotiator, but my normal speaking voice is very what you might call expressive. It goes up, it goes down, it goes all around. A regular audio show, my voice.

Do I use that when I'm talking? You betcha. The emotion in my voice—my enthusiasm, my empathy, my disbelief—they all underline what I'm saying. They're part of my personality when I'm talking, and they help me convey a sense of trust and build a rapport with the person on the other side of the negotiation.

I didn't consciously set out to develop a voice when I became a negotiator. It was already there. What I did do was realize that my voice modulated, and then trained myself to pay attention to what it said—the emotion beyond the content.

What was that slogan?

Know thyself? To thine ownself be true?

Takes one to know one?

A negotiator should know him- or herself. He should know how his voice sounds, and how her eyes reveal anger. Listen and watch yourself in action. Use the mirror, use videotape, use the shower if you have to—if you don't know what tools you have, you're not using them.

ROLE PLAYING

I encourage my students to practice and train to negotiate. I don't see why anyone who's interested in negotiating anything—a car purchase, a raise request, a date with Miss Universe—wouldn't want to take a few practice swings before stepping up to the plate. The best situation is to rehearse with someone else, as if you were practicing for a part in a play, but of course that's not always possible for a one-man or -woman negotiating team. You know what? Do it by yourself. Go ahead. In the bathroom, the kitchen, the office—just do it. Call it role playing, instead of talking to yourself, and it'll feel a lot more natural.

I believe that cassette and digital voice recorders are among the most helpful tools for training hostage negotiators. During my classes, I record students role playing and give them their own tapes to take home. Most students cannot believe the voice on the tape is them.

One caution here: If you do record your training sessions, take it easy on yourself. Listen to what you said, learn from how you reacted, make mental notes about your presentation style, but don't be too hard on yourself. We are our own worst critics, especially when we hear ourselves on tape. We always believe we could have done better.

DON'T BE HARD ON YOURSELF

Since we're on the topic, let's talk about criticism for just one more minute. Onlookers can and will criticize. It happens in all walks of life, and it certainly happens to negotiators. "I would have done this," they say. "He should have said that." The fact is, it's just too easy to criticize when you're not the one who had your butt in the hot seat and had to respond to a person holding hostages, with the lives of innocent people hanging on every word. Even if the negotiation didn't involve life and death, it's always easy to criticize. Negotiators shouldn't shut out constructive criticism, of course. But they should consider the source and remember that they were the ones who had their lives or livelihoods on the line. That's worth a lot more than armchair lip after the fact.

SUMMING UP

The most important words in any negotiation: *Talk to me.*

Emotions are an important part of communication. If you're just listening to the verbal content, you're not getting the entire message.

Negotiators shouldn't feel sorry for the person they're negotiating with—the goal is empathy, not sympathy.

Active listening means encouraging the other person to talk.

CHAPTER 6

THE FIRST YES

Establishing rapport
makes it possible to negotiate
when your life is on the line.

On February 11, 1993—shortly before I was hoping to retire from the NYPD, I might add—I happened to find myself at New York's Kennedy Airport. Up in the air overhead somewhere flew an airliner with over a hundred passengers aboard. Their lives were being threatened by a man holding a pistol to the pilot's head.

How the hell do you start a conversation with a guy like that?

For me, as nervous as I was—and believe me, I was pretty nervous—it was simple. I said, "What do you want me to call you?"

He hesitated.

I said, "Listen, I need a name."

"Call me Jack."

"Okay, Jack. I'm Dom. . . . Jack, I need to ask you something. During this, do you want me to lie to you, or do you want me to be honest and tell you the truth?"

"You better tell me the truth."

"That's all right, I want to be honest," I answered. "But you have to understand, it's possible that by being honest, I'm going to tell you something that's not what you want to hear. You have to promise me that that's okay and if that should happen you will not hurt anyone and you and I will work it out together. Is that okay?"

"Well yeah, all right. If you're going to be honest."

"You want me to be honest, right?"

"Yes."

From there, we had a basis to negotiate.

THE RIGHT YES

I stumbled on to that question—"Do you want me to be honest?"—and how powerful it was, early in my career as a negotiator. We had a tight situation, and I was just searching for something to say. I forget precisely what the guy on the other side of the door had said up to that point, but once I asked him the "Do you want me to lie to you?" question, his whole tone of voice changed. A light just about went off in my head: Everybody wants you to be honest with them. Get them to agree to honesty as the basis for your relationship, and you can negotiate anything. From that point on, that question—and attitude—were a standard part of my negotiating plan.

Salespeople often talk about getting the customer to say yes to something—anything—as an important step in the process of making a sale. Now I don't buy that entirely—I can say yes to a question about baseball and be no closer to buying a new suit than I was ten years ago when I bought my last one. But I do believe that the right "Yes" is an important step in getting negotiations going.

What I'm asking when I say, "Do you want me to be honest?" isn't whether the person wants me to lie or not—hell no, he doesn't want me lying; that's a no-brainer. What I'm saying is, "Are you ready to negotiate, or not?" If I tell you the truth, or at least what I think is the truth, are you going to look at it objectively, or at least try to? Can you and I work together to figure this thing out?

The question puts us on an even par. I can use it later on if I don't think the guy is leveling with me: "Hey, I'm telling you the truth, you gotta be square with me." I use his answer—and the rapport that it implied—to get him back to the table.

BUILDING RAPPORT

Everybody has their own style to get that first important yes, the first "right" yes. I'm not going to tell you what to say; if a real estate agent is negotiating with a potential client over the price of a house, it doesn't make sense to say, "Do you want me to be honest with you or lie to you?" What might work for her is something along the lines of: "Are you ready to buy, or do you need more information?"

"I need more information," says the potential buyer.

The real estate agent gives it. Now the key there is not—as real estate agents and buyers sometimes think—that the additional information represents an obligation to buy *that* house. That's misreading what's going on, even though quite a number of sales trainers will urge the salesman to phrase the question exactly that way because they think it makes it harder for the person to walk away. In their minds, the goal of getting that first yes and then giving the information is to sell that house.

It's not.

The goal of the first yes is to establish a rapport, a basis for negotiating. And negotiating is not closing. You negotiate all the points, then you close the deal.

The real estate agent provides information until the client is ready to start negotiations on that specific house. If the client is not interested in the house after the agent has done something for him or her, it isn't a lost sale, it's a postponed one—on a different house.

TAKING THE TIME TO SELL

When I was a kid, I noticed that some salespeople would let their customers talk their ears off. And I mean talk their ears off. Grandma So-and-so goes into the fabric store and spends a half hour talking with the owner about her grandkids: what they eat, what they read, what they burp . . . way too much information, if you get where I'm coming from.

Why was this woman wasting her time? Didn't she have anything better to do?

Maybe she did have other things to do, but she wasn't actually wasting her time. She was merely investing it in sales that day and in the future. There were, at the time, a half-dozen similar stores in the neighborhood. Grandma So-and-so came to that one because the owner cared about her. Listening meant that the person cared.

In hostage negotiations, the negotiator shows the other person that he cares all the time. It's part of building rapport. No words are wasted words; even the most innocuous comment can help you reach your goal. And a lot of this happens without a script.

YANKEE FANS

One of the funniest, maybe even most bizarre, examples I've ever seen of this happened during a New York hostage situation quite a number of years back. It was during the summer in an apartment house in New York, no AC out in the hallway, and if it was less than one hundred degrees in the stairwell where we all camped out, then I'm six-eight.

We have this situation with a subject locked inside an apartment with a weapon, and there's no phone, no way to communicate except shouting through the door. Literally.

And the subject is not exactly Mr. Sunshine.

So we go around and around for a while, everybody in full protective gear and behind ballistic shields, the whole shebang, sweat rolling down our backsides. Different members of the team take on the role of lead negotiator, only to meet with what is called "invective" in polite company. I think we all had a turn at trying to get this guy to talk, and did about as well as a single A minor league baseball player would do trying to get a hit against Pedro Martinez in his heyday. No rapport, no nothing except a hall full of sweat and four-letter words.

So into the middle of this steaming situation comes a new negotiator. It happens that it was his day off but he was in the neighborhood, and so he stopped by to see if he could help out. Even veterans do that, by the way; it wasn't like he was shining up to the commander or anything.

So he goes to the boss and says, "Mind if I give it a try?"

The commander figures, why not, it will give the other guys a break at least.

So the new negotiator puts on the vest, gets behind the ballistic shield, and waddles out there, trailing sweat along the floor.

"Hello inside, just wanted to say I'm out here blah-blah-blah."

The response began: "X#@#$#% you!" I'll leave the rest of that sentence to your imagination.

"Hey, not a problem," said the newbie. "I can't really hang around anyway. I got tickets to the game tonight, and I got to get going soon."

"Game? What game?"

"Yankee game."

"How'd you get tickets to that? It's been sold out for weeks."

"Oh, I got this buddy who knows somebody."

"You're really going to the Yankee game?"

"Yeah."

"They're going to win."

"I hope so. But the way Rivers is playing . . ."

"Ah, Rivers . . ."

Yeah, you guessed it. We're sweating our uniforms off, and these guys start talking about baseball. I guess the real highlight came when they started talking about baseball cards. Sheez.

"So listen, one Yankee fan to another, you want to come out of there?" said the negotiator finally.

"One fan to another, I'm coming out."

Unbelievable.

But it happened. They established a basis to negotiate via baseball, and then just about skipped over the negotiating part. Life should always be like that, right?

So here this guy is, on the floor, being cuffed, and the negotiator says, "Well listen, like I said, I'm going to come down with you to the station and go through the booking process with you, so no sweat."

Guy looks up and says, "Listen, man, don't miss that baseball game on account of me, okay? That's more important."

Only in New York.

IT AIN'T SMALL IF IT'S TALK

The point there—besides the total irrationality of baseball fans—is that there is no such thing as small talk in a negotiation. You need personal chatter to build a rapport. And sometimes it happens in just completely unpredictable and even bizarre ways.

Should every negotiation begin with baseball talk?

No. And frankly, I can do without any baseball talk, as my team is in the cellar this year. But you get the drift.

ZERO IN ON CONFLICTS

In hostage negotiations, sooner or later you have to bring up the difficult subject, to tell the guy: "You have to surrender, which means you're going to jail."

Now, we don't dwell on that second part in negotiating. The jail thing is not a real big plus, so we try to leave it in the background as much as possible. We don't deny it; we don't lie. But a negotiator is not under any obligation to advertise the downside of his proposed settlement. Besides, in most cases, we can safely assume that the guys on the other side of the barricade know that's the end result of surrendering.

I doubt that any business negotiation has as difficult a sticking point. After all, the alternative in most business situations is walking away and finding a deal elsewhere. In a hostage situation, the alternative to jail is a pine box with a whole bunch of dirt on top of you.

How do we deal with this difficult negotiating point, this conflict to end all conflicts?

Directly. One of the first questions we usually ask after we've established rapport is simply: "Will you come out?"

You do get some interesting responses the first time you ask it, I'll admit. Although, more than one suspect has simply laid down his weapon at that point and come out, hands exactly where we've told them to be.

Mostly, surrender is a difficult issue you come back to over and over. As everyday negotiations proceed, difficult points tend to accumulate. They become the heart of the negotiation—and the basis of the deal. You work on these issues—"problems" sounds a bit negative, no?—and create a solution.

A win-win solution, if you like the trendy terminology.

US, NOT THEM

In building his rapport with the subject, a hostage negotiator has created an "us" working on a problem together. If there's a "them," it's the commander—the guy who's making the decision—and the ninjas with the guns, who represent the alternative to the decision. When we look at that last difficult issue facing us, we're working on it together.

Look, I don't own the guy's problems, just like he doesn't own mine. (Though there have been a few situations where I was tempted to trade, believe it or not.) But they're tangential to the issue of his surrendering. They may help—maybe he can start to deal with his problems after he surrenders, goes to counseling, gets a better divorce lawyer, whatever. During the negotiations, we're focused on the issue; his problems—or needs—are of interest in working on that issue.

And we can always work it out together.

Given that you can adopt this kind of attitude in the most hostile situation imaginable, you know it's possible in a business situation. Successful negotiators try to arrange solutions for the difficult issues that are win-win. Now that doesn't necessarily mean that both sides get everything they want, or even are 100 percent happy. But if the negotiators can meet each other's needs by working on those difficult issues together, they have a basis to close the deal.

THE TERMINAL OR THE PRESS

Let's go back to my 1992 hijacker for an example of working together on an issue. The hijacker turned out to have two demands, and only two demands. Number one, he wanted to surrender at the Lufthansa terminal. And number two, he wanted no media around.

Now the commander had zero problem with number two. In fact, he wanted nobody around for the surrender. Heck, if it were possible, we wouldn't even have had cops there—anybody close enough to see what's going on is close enough to get hurt. But the Lufthansa terminal was a problem, basically because it would be very difficult to keep innocent people away and guarantee that they wouldn't be hurt. We could evacuate it, but even so, a surrender there would be much more dangerous than in an isolated area elsewhere on the airport complex.

So what do I do?

I get on the line and I say, "Jack, I've been working on the issues you requested, and we have a small problem I need to discuss with you. The international terminal is so large that it would be impossible to keep all the press away. I may have a solution, though, if you want to hear it. Maybe we can work it out."

"Let me hear it."

"There's a VIP area that the president uses and people like that. We can guarantee that there would be no press there. What about it?"

He thought about it for a few minutes, then warned me that I better not be planning a trick. I assured him that I was keeping my end of the bargain. He thought about it for a few seconds more—and let me tell you, those few seconds seemed like hours—and then agreed.

WHAT'D I DO?

So what did I do? I presented it as an issue that we could both work on. I used his needs to find a good, viable solution.

Now there was definitely subtle stuff going on. I deemphasized my position and played up his, knowing from the emotional information I picked up earlier which of the two points was more important for him. I did take a little bit of a risk, because it was possible that he could have said, "You know what, let the press in—I want my mug on the front page of the *Post* tomorrow." But the risk was fairly small compared to the payoff: surrender in an isolated and easily controlled area.

WIN-WIN NEVER REALLY IS

The whole give-and-take thing, the idea of win-win, people working together, dissecting an issue—all that stuff is true, but it only comes after you've built a rapport. You have to be in a position to:

- Know exactly what it is the other side wants.

- Know exactly what it is you want.

- Have some trust that you and your opposite number are working on an even playing field.

If you have that, then you can feel comfortable enough to take the small risks you need to make the give-and-take work. Because win-win doesn't happen in the real world. In the real world it's more like, kinda win–not lose. Or kinda win–kinda kinda win. Or not really lose–not really lose.

Giving up something you want, or at least think you want, is usually an important step to reaching your goal in a negotiation. And so is risk. The thing to remember is that you're never giving up your alternative—the ninjas at your back, Plan B.

SUMMING UP

I build rapport in a hostage situation with a simple question that does many things: "Do you want me to be honest with you?" It's the first yes, and it helps build the rapport and trust you need to negotiate.

Negotiations take time.

Sometimes the oddest turns lead to the best results.

To reach a deal, you almost always have to give up something, or at least risk doing so.

Losing a little to gain a lot is perfectly acceptable.

CHAPTER 7

IS HE A PSYCHO, OR JUST A MANIAC?

Knowing what kind of crazy you're dealing with can help you tailor your negotiating approach.

Can you tell me exactly what being crazy means?

I've been in this business for a long time but I still can't answer that question. I know there are medical terms and conditions and definitions, but "crazy" is one of those things that's just, well, crazy to define.

On one particular cold night the negotiation team I was working was called to deal with a man threatening suicide in an apartment in Brooklyn. The ninjas had the man cornered in a bedroom. The man weighed about 400 pounds and was armed with a twelve-inch butcher knife. He threatened to kill anyone who came into the room. He also yelled about people out to kill him and how he trusted no one and he was going to take his own life before someone else did. Because of the way the apartment was laid out and the fact that there was no phone in the room where he was, I had to do the type of negotiation I dread the most: face-to-face.

Or rather, face-to-very-big-knife.

If it were not for the eight ninjas around me and the Kevlar vest and helmet I wore, I'm not entirely sure I would have gone in. I know for a fact I would have rather been out fishing. And for the record, I should say that hostage negotiators are actually trained and instructed and drilled on *not* getting in exactly that sort of situation.

But anyway, I was trying to calm the subject down and getting nowhere. He kept yelling over me, and my words were lost in all the noise. I decided to do something that was different for me at the time, since I was still fairly new to the field: I just shut up and listened.

The man's yelling went on for what seemed like hours—and I know he did a thirty-minute stretch without stopping to take a breath. As I listened I started to hear what was going on inside his distraught mind. He was in pain. Not physical pain, but deep emotional pain. He was scared and felt alone. It seems easy now to point this out, as if of course that's what was going on, but I really didn't understand it when I walked into the room. It was a big knife, after all, and a very loud rant.

As soon as he stopped his ranting, I took the opportunity to get my word in: "I can hear from what you are saying that you are in pain. You are hurting and feel alone."

Bring on my Ph.D. He looked at me as if he was trying to figure out exactly who I was and was I for real. I continued to talk with a soothing calm voice, and we could all see this very big dangerous man start to deflate like someone had just let the air out of him. I assured him that I would tell the doctors about his pain. A calm came over him like a security blanket, and he dropped the knife and walked into the arms of the ninjas.

I knew this time that it was dangerous, because our big teddy bear could turn into a very big dangerous problem. Was he crazy? Was he a maniac?

Tell you the truth, I have no idea. The one thing I do know is that he needed help and I was lucky enough to stumble on the right words.

RIGHT MINDS

I'm thinking this goes without saying, but as a general rule your average hostage taker is not entirely in his right mind. Or at least what most of us would consider our right minds.

But here's a question for you: How many people do you think are "sane"? I mean, no one's completely normal, except you and I, of course.

But within the established parameters of sanity, how many people do you figure are eating a full bowl of cornflakes in the morning?

According to the FBI statistics I've seen, only 70 percent of the population is normal. The rest are psychotics or have personality disorders.

Seventy percent. That means three out of the next ten people you meet are missing a couple of playing cards. Maybe that will help you keep your perspective as you navigate rush hour traffic on the way to work tomorrow.

PERSONALITIES COUNT

In my opinion, a good negotiator uses his or her personality during the negotiation. If he's an easygoing guy, he'll take a relaxed approach, talking in ways that are comfortable to him, probably BS'ing for a bit before getting to the actual meat of the issue. If she's all business and likes to get quickly to the bullet point, then she should do that during the negotiating process.

All personalities complicate negotiations in their own way. Changing your personal style when you negotiate isn't practical. And everyone has to negotiate at some point in their lives. The issue may not be nuclear proliferation, but negotiating a curfew is still negotiating—and sometimes nearly as hazardous.

And just as your personality is important, so is the personality of the guy or gal on the other side of the line. It's important to understand the personality of the person you're dealing with as you negotiate, because their particular bent plays a role in the process. Someone who is a narcissist egotist who thinks his pits smell like Chanel No. 5 ought to be treated differently than someone who is paranoid.

One little caution here: Don't get too hung up on the following labels. You're not giving the guy on the other side of the table a personality test, and you sure as hell are not interested in straightening out his head. All the negotiating team wants to do is negotiate. Knowing roughly where the guy is coming from—what parts of his personality are so beyond his control that they're part of his negotiating technique—is enough. You want a psych degree, you go to college.

And besides, even with all the wonderful meds they have for psychos these days, it's still hard as hell to get them to take them.

THE FOUR TYPES OF HOSTAGE TAKERS

At the NYPD we used to break down hostage takers into four broad categories:

- Professional criminals who found themselves trapped after trying to escape from a crime.

- Emotionally disturbed individuals—a catchall category for everyone from a paranoid schizophrenic to a severely depressed person.

- People involved in domestic incidents, possibly the most unpredictable of all. These incidents involve people who know each other and in many cases are married or living together.

- Terrorists—groups driven by distorted beliefs, be they political, religious, or ethnic. The common perception is that the police or government does not negotiate with a terrorist, but that's not necessarily true.

PROFESSIONAL CRIMINALS AND TERRORISTS

As a general rule, professional criminals tend to be the easiest people to deal with. They know the drill and have very clear and identifiable goals—usually getting out of the situation with a minimum of hassle. Someone who robs a bank and then gets trapped inside usually will be able to recognize how hopeless his or her situation is and will eventually begin dealing with the negotiator on a more or less rational basis.

At the other extreme, terrorists rarely are willing to deal with you on a rational basis. Many are motivated by religion or politics, or a little of both. In many cases, death is not the worst thing that could happen to them. Our strategy for dealing with them usually involves hoping that their resolve fades as time goes on. Self-preservation, fortunately, is a strong biological instinct.

DOMESTIC DISPUTES

Domestic incidents are the most unpredictable negotiations because they are driven by emotion. These usually involve people who are married, living together, or are family members. The fact that these incidents are driven by emotions rather than greed or religious belief makes them extremely dangerous. More police officers are hurt and injured each year handling domestic and family disputes than any other call they respond to. A hostage taking where the taker is emotionally connected to the hostage makes for a very bad mix. During these incidents it is very common for the hostage taker to degrade his hostage (usually his wife or girlfriend) in every way possible.

One of the most important things that negotiators have to do here is reinstate the hostage's dignity in the eyes of the hostage taker. The negotiator cannot qualify or join in with the hostage taker's feelings toward his captive. This is certainly not the time to show the taker empathy by telling him, "I know exactly how you feel, I have one just like her at home."

Even if you do!

Hey, just kidding. Lighten up.

BREAKING IT DOWN

I handled an incident one evening where a man was holding his common-law wife hostage. This guy was most certainly not the kind of guy you would want to marry your sister or even walk your dog. We had intelligence on him that told us the police were called to this location regularly and that he'd been arrested in the past for beating the woman he was holding. This time, though, when the police showed up at his door thinking they were going to handle the situation as usual, they found out differently. Our subject opened the door holding his wife around the throat with one arm. With his other hand he held a gun to her head.

My first contact with this model of society was rather interesting. As I was going over in my head what I would say, I heard his phone ring and he answered. Before I could even get out a hello, he started yelling at me about how he would kill her and that she was useless and should die. Hell, all I was looking for was "Hello."

I asked my new best friend, "How is Mary doing?" This brought a new round of yelling and degrading comments about his wife. Each time he went into a rampage about Mary, I used a soft but determined voice to tell him that it was not nice to talk about Mary that way. I explained that even though they had problems in their relationship, there were other ways he could handle it. The goal at this point was just to get him to see Mary as a real person. Hostage takers who degrade their captives and refuse to recognize them as human beings worthy of respect and proper treatment are basically saying, "You are not worthy to live. You are a nonentity, and no one would care if I give you what you deserve." The hostage taker is convincing himself that it's okay to hurt his captive. The most important goal at this point is to reverse that process.

I won't bore you with all two hours of the back and forth, but it was basically volley and serve, volley and serve—she's a useless witch, she is not. Is, is not.

Finally I asked that simple question again: "How is Mary doing?"

This time his reply came in a sullen voice: "Mary is okay. She's sitting on the couch."

We all looked at each other and knew this was a major breakthrough—he'd actually started to see her as a person again. About another two hours later he released Mary and then surrendered himself.

Okay, Dominick, the story is great, but what the hell does it have to do with business?

The point is, in an unpredictable situation—or a very complicated negotiation—sometimes it's easier to break the goal down into different parts or steps, and negotiate toward step one first. Had I started right in trying to get the hostage taker out, it's likely that the negotiation would have floundered and Mary would have been shot if not killed. It's important to recognize a potentially complicated situation from the outset and plan your tactics accordingly.

Most negotiations are based on a multitude of small accomplishments. Yeah, we would all love to go in at 8 a.m. and sit at the corporate meeting table for a major contract negotiation, have a cup of coffee, and be on our way by 8:45 with a signed contract. Real life is hard work, with a little luck thrown in on the side. Determination, sweat, and long, long hours—that's what really leads to success.

Oh, by the way, if I was able to perfect that, go in at 8:00 and get out at 8:45 with a great contract, I would not be writing this book while in a plane 34,000 feet up.

Well, maybe I would—but it would be *my* plane.

DEALING WITH PROS

In everyday negotiations, the easiest people to deal with are the people who negotiate all the time. This may seem like a contradiction. Most of us think that if we're up against someone who's a pro, we're going to get ripped off. I guarantee you've felt that way if you've ever stepped foot on a car lot.

But the truth is, a professional knows the drill beforehand. As long as you've done your homework, you're no more likely to get screwed by him or her than you are by Joe Blow off the street. Now that doesn't mean you're going to kick his butt up and down the soccer field—but that isn't your goal anyway. If you're looking at the negotiation process to boost your ego—if you're keeping score—you may very well get your pocket picked by a skilled pro. Because he'll just play to your ego. Stroke, stroke, stroke.

The commander sets the goal before you begin your negotiations. That is the yardstick to use, not how many jabs you land. It's not boxing, or even professional wrestling.

THE IMPORTANCE OF PROFESSIONALISM

The key to dealing with a pro is to come off as someone who has done their homework. You don't have to pretend you're as good a negotiator as they are—this isn't an ego thing. But if you demonstrate early on that you know what you want, and you're serious about negotiating, then any pro worth his or her salt will take you seriously.

And if they don't?

Your best bet is to find someone who will.

Here's another buddy story, and this one involving car sales, which seem to make more people nervous than just about any other area they negotiate in.

Friend goes into a car dealership that is having one of those twenty-four-hour sale-a-thon things. He already knows which model he wants, and in fact has already spoken to another dealer and knows roughly how much he'd have to pay to get the model he wants. Finds a salesman, gives him a little bit of background on what he wants. Salesman right away tries to steer him to another model.

"No, I want a Maxima SE," he says. "And I want leather." And blah-blah-blah, whatever other stuff he's into. I may have the model wrong there, and some of the blah-blah-blah may have been yadda-yadda-yadda, but you get the idea.

Salesman says, "Well, I can't do leather as an option, but I can do after-market leather."

My friend was savvy enough to recognize that was a complete BS line: He not only knew from research that leather was a viable option, but had also scouted around enough to know that after-market leather is a notorious area, worse even than after-sales warranties and rust-proofing. (Spare me, please.) When the salesman told him that, the salesman was really saying: "I'm not taking you seriously." Now, since my friend had already signaled that he knew what he wanted and had done some research—he was able to name the packages that were offered with the model—he concluded that the salesman wasn't really a pro.

My friend's a generous guy when it comes to assessing character.

So what did he do? Two things: He decided he wasn't going to buy a car there, since the dealer didn't care enough about his cars and reputation to properly train its salesmen.

And he asked to talk to the sales manager.

Not to complain, but to get a real deal.

In short order, the sales manager—who *was* a real pro—cut through the BS and gave my friend what under other circumstances would have been an excellent price. (Let's call it $200 under invoice, which was a good deal in this case, though you and I know those invoice numbers are baloney, right?) He then had that price to use back with the other dealer—also a pro—as he nailed down the deal. And incidentally, he was willing to pay a higher price at the other dealer because the negotiator (read "salesman") took a professional attitude. His interpretation was that the negotiator simply reflected the attitude of management, and that if anything went wrong with the car down the line, he wanted to be dealing with professionals.

He didn't pay a higher price, but he would have. At least that's what he says now.

REAL LIFE: EMOTIONALLY DISTURBED PEOPLE

Of course, you don't always have the option of negotiating with a pro. When hostage negotiators find themselves dealing with a person of unbalanced brain—or worse, a terrorist—we try to remember that time is on our side. We don't actually wait for someone to achieve enlightenment or get their act together. But as a general rule, resolve weakens over time. And in the case of chemically driven insanity, the craziness also may fade.

As an everyday negotiator, you're unlikely to deal with real crazies—and if you happen to run into them, you probably will be able to run away. But a touch of insanity comes free of charge with every personality type. So while the following labels are extreme, at least one of them will apply in some way to most people you deal with in life.

PARANOID SCHIZOPHRENICS

According to the studies, the two most common whackos—that would be the technical term for people with "abnormal personalities"—involved in hostage-taking incidents are psychotics and those with personality disorders.

Hostage negotiators break down psychotics into two different groups, basically because our tactics for dealing with them are very different. Paranoid schizophrenics are people who see the world through different eyes than the rest of us. They have false mental perceptions—very possibly seeing and hearing things that we don't—and generally think they're being persecuted.

Of course, that last perception may have some basis in fact after the tactical squad arrives, since they are surrounded by people with guns. But it does make it difficult to build rapport.

The first thing we try to find out is whether such a person is on meds, and if so, whether they've taken them. We try very hard not to do anything to reinforce their paranoia—hands in full view, if you have to deal with them face-to-face. And we never argue with them about their delusions. We tell them we understand that they see things, though we don't.

In a sense, everybody you deal with in a negotiation is a paranoid schizophrenic—they see a different world than you do. Do what a hostage negotiator does: Don't argue with them about their worldview. You're not there to change it. Let them tell you from their perspective what they see. Listen to their needs, then use them as you work together on the difficult issue or issues that the negotiation involves.

ANTISOCIAL PERSONALITIES

Most criminals have antisocial personalities; that's why they're criminals. They don't get along with society. They refuse to play by the rules, they're selfish, irresponsible, and rarely feel guilt. If something goes wrong, they blame others, never themselves. They tend to be hostile and unreliable.

It's hard to work out a deal with such people. On the one hand, you have to be careful not to challenge or threaten their ego. On the other hand, if you appear weak, you'll never get a deal done with them. They'll try to bully you and take advantage, and then just as you think you've got it worked out—oops, that wasn't what they were thinking at all, not at all.

The parallel I find in everyday negotiations is the bullying type, the person who likes to think he's a tough nut to crack and he's not going to give an inch. This type can be a pain to negotiate with. They tend to be stubborn and unresponsive to your needs. They see negotiation as a zero-sum game: They get all the marbles, you get none.

Obviously, I'm assuming here that you do actually need or at least want what it is he has. If you don't, there's no sense wasting your time with them.

In dealing with this type, avoid turning the negotiations into a battle of egos. Negotiations are supposed to be win-win, not winner takes all. If you play their game, you're probably going to lose—if you actually do make a deal at all. Demands issued harshly are a bad idea in any event, but with this type they are only going to make the person dig in harder.

When a hostage negotiator is speaking with someone who's antisocial, we avoid talking about punishment and we don't parade our tactical squad in front of the windows. We don't say "My way or the highway." We try to show only that the deal is in the person's best interest. In effect, we use his ego against him—we want him to think he's won.

Obviously, you can only do this in a negotiation if your ego is not attached to the tactics you're using. If you don't see the negotiation as a contest, then you're not going to get hung up in that.

At some point when you're dealing with this type of negotiator, you're going to want to make a point of letting them score some points. You may even emphasize the points they raised that you agreed to. Of course, you are not going to agree to anything that you weren't prepared to in the first place—right?

That's because the commander set the goal and figured out what you were willing to give up in order to reach it ahead of time. The person on the other side doesn't have to know that you were fully prepared to eat the delivery costs on the piano as part of the deal. What he *does* need to know is that he asked you to do that and you agreed. Reluctantly, of course. And only because of his skill as a negotiator. Because the guy is obviously a genius.

DON'T BE BULLIED

The real trick when you're negotiating with this type of person is holding on to your main positions and making concessions elsewhere without looking like a wimp. Because if he thinks you're a wimp, it's going to take forever for him to realize you're not.

You're not. Trust me.

And keep reminding yourself that it's not personal. Tactics are fluid. Your goal—your bottom line, the thing you've decided you want and what you're willing to pay/do in exchange for it—carefully figured out by the commander before the negotiations began, is not personal.

Convincing the other side that you're not going to cave in can be done partly through body language and voice tone. You should always appear confident and knowledgeable during your negotiations, but it's especially important in this case. It's not a weakness to admit you don't know something or will have to check on it; it's all in how you do it.

If you go, "Uh, um, well by, uh, golly I never thought of that, and, uh well, I don't know . . ." the wimp light will begin blinking above your head.

But if you say, "You know, you may have a good point there. Let me research that and get back to you," you've done several things. Besides complimenting the other side on his intelligence without yourself looking bad, you've set the stage to say, "Now let's move on to point B . . ."

INADEQUATE PERSONALITIES

There's a perception that all criminals are egotists who think they're better than everyone else. There certainly are those, but there's also a good hunk who have what shrinks call a weak self-image. These folks generally can't respond effectively to emotional and social demands. They don't necessarily fall apart, but they don't respond in a reliable manner.

In everyday situations, inadequate personalities come off as being slightly hysterical and unsure of themselves. Hostage negotiators deal with them by going heavy on ego support and giving them a way out of the situation. People with a weak ego need direction, and they need stroking to back up that direction. We will often point out that they're facing overwhelming odds, and we'll emphasize the fact that the ninjas are out there. But as we talk to them about the alternatives to the ninjas, we try to make the subject see that the alternative benefits them.

What they often need is a face-saving way of surrendering. They have weak egos to begin with, so if you can give them a way to boost their ego slightly, they won't feel as if they're backing down.

BORDERLINES AND
OTHER EMOTIONAL TYPES

I avoid psychiatric jargon as a general rule, but let me throw an official personality disorder at you for discussion's sake. The psychological profession has long known of—and usually tried to avoid—a type of person said to have "borderline personality disorder." There's a lot of controversy among counselors about the disorder and the diagnosis, but in general we're talking about a person whose every interaction is a full-blown emotional crisis. They're either way in love with someone or way in hate with them—and those extremes may be only five minutes apart. They seem agreeable to a fault on Monday, and find fault with everything including the spelling of your name on Tuesday.

Sound a little like your last girlfriend?

Borderline personalities are tough to deal with because their emotions are so far off the scale. Their actions and decisions are based on how they feel—not on their actual goals. A successful negotiator will therefore be aware of the person's emotions, and focus on them. "How do you feel about point x-y-z?" works with that sort of person because how they feel is more important than the point itself.

The trick, though, is not to try to cure those emotions. Remember—you don't own the other side's problem, or his needs and values. You try to use them to work on the difficult issues that block the deal. Resolve the issues, get him out of the building, and let him fix his problems himself.

I DUNNO

Have you ever tried to keep a two-year-old happy? Most days you can do it with a few toys and maybe a silly song or two, but then there are days when nothing works. In desperation, you ask the child, "What do you want?"

And the kid says, "I dunno."

I dunno is the hardest issue to deal with in negotiations. If you're talking with someone who doesn't know what they want, you have no basis for negotiating. You don't have closure, you don't have anything meaningful to talk about. All you have is a whining two-year-old.

In everyday negotiating, people who don't know what they want are simply not ready to negotiate. You shouldn't be in that position yourself—because you've done your homework, right? But even the best prepared negotiating team is going to occasionally find itself in a situation where it's dealing with issues it hadn't considered before the session began.

Once again, the team approach becomes important here—the negotiator gives way to the intelligence officer, who gathers more information and presents it to the commander. On a one-man team, you drop into explore mode and gather intelligence, asking questions—just remember that's what you're doing, getting intelligence, not negotiating.

DICTATING TERMS

What happens if the other side really doesn't know what it wants?

It'll be tempting, very tempting, to simply dictate terms . . . or to try to throw them in as oh-by-the-ways at the closing.

Don't do it.

The basis of good negotiating is mutual trust and understanding. That's not just feel-good baloney socks either. Going into a negotiation, negotiators should have a clearly defined goal. Achieving that goal is what it's all about. Skipping over the fine print makes you vulnerable to it at the closing.

Now I'm not saying you have to bend over backward to help the other side, or that you should emphasize the negatives of a deal for the other side. If I'm talking with a hostage taker who's already committed a murder, I'm not likely to say something like, "Well you know, after you surrender we will be hoping to fry you in the electric chair."

But you do owe it to yourself to present a fair and equitable deal.

To *yourself!*

Yup. Because it's very possible that the people you're dealing with will wake up tomorrow, and if not then, the day after that, and if they feel they've been ripped off, they may back out of the deal. If it's too late for that, they may still find some way to get back at you—if only by refusing to do business with you again.

Call it Dominick's rule of complete negotiations: Major issues in a contract should always be aired at the negotiation stage. If the other side doesn't bring them up, make sure you do.

A PSYCHO, OR A MANIAC?

A psycho is someone who is certifiably insane. They're mentally unbalanced and belong under a doctor's care.

But a maniac is a little different. A maniac is someone who may act a little crazy, a little out of control, but falls within the general parameters of mental stability. She may do crazy things, but she'll ace the Rorschach test every time.

Maniacs negotiate all the time. They generally announce their style by making outrageous demands and doing things to break up the negotiating flow. Demands, even outrageous ones, are not a problem; we'll get into dealing with them in more detail in the next chapter.

If you're dealing with people who act like maniacs, the most important thing to remember is that it's part of a strategy. It's not a particularly effective one, since at best it's wasting time and at worst it's pissing you off. But it's a strategy, and not a comment on your goal.

Probably not theirs either. Ask them what they really want, what's important to them in the negotiations. Counter with your actual points. If they're still acting out—to use shrink lingo—a short time-out may be in order.

What you don't want to do is play maniac back. It may be fun, it may even feel good, but it usually doesn't help you get back to your goal.

GETTING EMOTIONAL

All right, truth telling time: I can't always take my own advice. Even I have been known to play the maniac back.

One time during a negotiation, I had a real hard case in a room with an old lady. On the phone, he started going off about what he was going to do to her, and at some point I just snapped back: "If you hurt one little gray hair on her head, I will be the one to ID your body in the morgue today."

It was a completely emotional response; it was absolutely not what you're trained to do. It's not what I was trained to do, and I certainly wouldn't recommend it as a way to introduce yourself.

But it did actually work. I had a moment of controlled craziness. And the hostage taker responded instantly with, "She's okay. She's sitting on the couch." That was the last time he threatened her safety, and five hours later he released her unharmed.

I can justify it now: I had a feeling that if I just kept letting him spew the venom, he was going to talk himself into slitting her throat. It comes under the category of using your personality and your emotions, and in that way it complies with the rules, not breaks them.

Still, I was a bit of a psycho that moment.

See? Everybody's a little crazy.

A CHANGE IN TACTICS

Sane people who use insane tactics as part of their shtick usually will drop those tactics when they realize they're not working. Outrageous behavior and demands have a tendency to disintegrate when it becomes obvious that the real goal is obtainable without them.

Again, you're not out to fix the person's head, just to make a deal. That's where the focus of the negotiations should be.

SUMMING UP

Everybody's a little nuts when it comes to negotiations. Be prepared to deal with different personality types differently—change your tactics, not your goals.

Never be afraid of dealing with a professional negotiator. If you've done your homework, pros are the easiest people to work with.

The key to not being bullied: Know your goal before you get into the situation, and stick to it. Keep separation between the negotiator and the commander. This way, if the negotiator *is* bullied, a bad decision won't result.

Cover all important points in the negotiation stage, even if the other side doesn't.

CHAPTER 8

THE TWO Ds: DEMANDS AND DEADLINES

To the skilled negotiator, demands and deadlines are like diamonds: your best friends.

Most people tend to get paranoid about two things in negotiations: demands and deadlines. Hostage negotiators are trained never to use those two words. We avoid talking about deadlines—ours or theirs—and we don't make demands. We have points that are non-negotiable, of course; we're never going to give the bad guy a gun, for instance. But we don't present them as demands. We don't need to make the people we're dealing with any more squirrelly than they already are.

On the other hand, we welcome both demands and deadlines. They are valuable tools as we work toward a resolution in the negotiating crisis. If the other side gives you a list of demands—they won't use that word, of course—and a deadline, jump for joy.

DEMANDS: A DIRTY WORD

Demands is a very ugly word. It makes rational people act irrationally.

Don't believe me? Go into a store and yell, "I demand satisfaction!" and notice how many different shades the salespeople's faces turn.

Then go down to the other end of the mall and say, "Can you help me?" and see if there's a difference.

Most negotiators realize that the word *demand* is too loaded to use in a serious negotiation. That doesn't mean they won't present them. They'll use words that are easier to take, like *wants* or *needs* or even *points* or *items*. As a general rule, the more neutral the term you use to outline your position, the better off you are. Hostage negotiators generally present their own position passively: as a reaction to what the other guy does. We don't have demands, but we do have non-negotiable points:

- The hostage taker never gets a gun.

- We never add to the hostages.

- We never release people who are in jail or otherwise in legal custody.

As a general rule, we make these positions known as we answer requests by the subject. Which psychologically makes them easier for the other side to discuss. Not necessarily to accept, of course, but at least to discuss.

GIVE SOMETHING FOR SOMETHING

If you don't call demands *demands,* then it's easier to realize that meeting them can give you leverage in the negotiations. Call them *needs.* Meeting another person's needs is a good thing: I meet your needs, you meet mine, we have a relationship going here, and it's mutually beneficial.

Fulfilling the other side's needs is the basis for fulfilling your own. It's what the process is really all about.

But it's give-and-take, tit-for-tat, one hand washing the other—take your favorite cliché and sticker it at the top of your notepad.

In hostage negotiations, we always give something for something. You want food, okay, good, I got food on the way—pizza, heroes, some of the best doughnuts this side of Krispy Kreme. I'll meet your need, now you meet mine: Give me six of your hostages. Something for something.

Don't get too hung up on the balance: one thing for one thing, two-for-two, etc. I think it's better to keep it looser, like you're not really keeping track.

122

But of course you are. If the other side starts balking or even runs out of needs, that's not a problem: Remind them how much you've already given.

"I'll take less of a raise than we both agree I'm worth, but in exchange for that, I really need . . ."

"I'm going to work my butt off to meet your deadline, but it's going to cost me with my wife. To keep her happy, I have to build that into the price. . . ."

And on and on. Something for something. Successful negotiations are two-sided, mutual benefit operations. Demands are just a chance to make that happen.

GOING FIRST

There's a game negotiators often play called "You go first." You see it a lot in negotiations involving money, where it's generally believed that the first person to actually mention a price loses. If a salesman says Auto X goes for $40,000, the prospective customer is not going to offer to pay more.

Now I realize that as a practical matter, the first person to mention a figure does set out the general parameters of the deal. And as a hostage negotiator, I'm used to being in the reactive mode. The words, "What exactly is it you want?" are not stapled to my lip only because they're tattooed to my tongue.

But here's the deal: It's okay to go first. It's okay to put a number out in the air. Realize that's what you're doing. Know that you're setting the parameters of the discussion. And take it from there. A few times you may shock the other side because your offer is far higher (or far lower) than they were hoping for. But if you did your research properly, you know how much the thing is actually worth anyway. The odds are that they'll eventually find out; you're better off in the long run being fair.

And really, what is the downside? You're our car salesman, you offered first to go $500 over invoice. The other side was prepared to pay more but now comes in a little lower, and the deal is still done.

You didn't just sell him a car and make $400 plus the hold back and yadda-yadda-yadda. You also got him blabbing about what a great deal he got from the local Ford place. The $100 you supposedly lost will come back several times over in the form of his friends walking through the door.

NUMBER PSYCHOLOGY

Whether you're an amateur or an experienced negotiator, you realize that most people are not going to make their first offer their last, at least not when you're dealing with money. That makes it easier to go first and shoot high or low; you can always backtrack.

I'm not going to tell you that you can't break that rule—there are certainly circumstances when you should, and if your personality is one shot and out, then go for it. But if you do intend on breaking it, make very clear, very very clear, that the figure is not going to be negotiated. Say, "This is my final number," or words to that effect. Not, "I thought I'd pay this."

Which brings us to a general rule about making demands: If it's non-negotiable, say so when you bring it up. Save yourself the hassle of a long-drawn-out test; suffer only a shorter one instead.

But be very comfortable with your out, because you may have to take it.

CRUMPLING THEM UP

Most times when people make demands—whether they use that word or not—they're simply starting negotiations off. A list of demands is simply something to talk about.

And most demands, frankly, are bullshit.

If I'm known for anything outside of police and negotiating circles, it's the negotiation I was involved in at New York City's Kennedy Airport, where a hijacker had threatened to blow up a Lufthansa airliner if his demands weren't met. The way the media had it, I took the list of demands the hijacker had, crumpled them up dramatically and confidently, and said, "Let's start from scratch."

Well, the media was wrong. I may have looked confident, but I was nervous as hell.

But I did crumple up the demands. I don't advise that as a general rule in a negotiation—it can really piss people off—but in this case I did it to make a point. The demands weren't just bullshit. They were a set of pre-conceived notions that were so far off the board, just so outrageous, that we couldn't even use them to talk about. The hijacker wanted to fly out of JFK, wanted prisoners released, may even have wanted the poor of India and Africa fed, for all I know—like I said, I tossed them so I can't get them and check.

And incidentally, it turned out later that the demands weren't even the hostage taker's. The FBI had come up with the list from . . . well, to be honest, I'm still not sure where.

Which is the first rule of dealing with demands: Make sure they come from the other side, and not your own assumptions.

You have to ask what the other side wants.

Otherwise you don't know.

Which was what I did next in that negotiation. And instead of some long list covering everything from freeing criminals to feeding the poor, the demands came back as two things:

1.   I want to surrender at the Lufthansa terminal.

2.   I do not want my picture taken. If I see the press there, people will get hurt.

We talked a bit more than that, but basically that's where we went. You can see right away that those demands are a heck of a lot more tangible than feeding the hungry of the world, though I don't deny that feeding the hungry does have a certain nobility to it. Those are demands—*needs,* if you will—that can be worked on together and solved.

SEPARATION OF POWERS

Finding out what the other side wants is the negotiator's job. Acting on it is the commander's.

That's one important reason we don't let a police chief take the negotiator role. Because once presented with the demand, he would have to immediately act on it one way or the other. It's logical, right? He's the one in charge: If he's got the power to decide, then how can he not decide?

The negotiator, on the other hand, can take a more neutral role, listening to the demands and passing them on. Physically, after I ask a person what they want, I take out a pen and paper and write it down. And I make sure they know that's what I'm doing.

Why?

Because I want them to understand that I'm taking their demands or points or interests, or whatever word we're using that day, seriously. I may think that 95 percent of all demands are baloney, but the signal I send back is one of respect for the person who's making them.

It also shows that the demands—needs, whatever—are things that are outside the person, and outside me. I have a list on paper that I can take to the guy in charge to discuss. I'm letting the person on the other side of the barricade see my process.

A little. I want him to understand that I'm not the commander. I'm working with him, and he and I are going to solve this thing together.

OUTRAGEOUS DEMANDS

Really whacko demands tend to get pushed aside as the negotiations go on. In a hostage situation, the more outrageous points may be mentioned once and then completely forgotten. That's not always true in everyday negotiations. An outrageous delivery date on a special order may actually be important to the person who's making the demand. If there's any question at all, you have to bring the issue back up at some point. That's because outrageous demands that are real, as opposed to baloney, have the potential to be deal breakers. They're the difficult issues that stand in the way of an agreement, and the spot where most negotiations that fail eventually bog down.

Of course, negotiations that succeed also bog down there, but no one seems to mind about that.

There are two schools of thought on when to deal with the most difficult parts of a negotiation: up front (after establishing rapport) and at the end. I'll lay out the thinking for each; the decision on which to use is up to you.

UP FRONT

The idea with bringing up a deal breaker early on is usually simple: If you can't get that delivery date, there's no sense talking about anything else. Someone can promise you a million dollars to design their Web site, but if it has to literally be done yesterday, you're just wasting your time talking about it. The usual approach here will be something along the lines of: "Well, let's talk about that deadline, because that's really important to me."

Investing time in the most difficult problem up front tends to make the rest of the process smoother, assuming you can work out the issue. Getting a resolution sets the basis for a final deal, and since you've already discussed your most important point or points, by definition you've achieved your goal.

But there are pitfalls to be aware of. One is tactical: If you've shot your wad on this issue, you may have very little left to give as the negotiating process turns to other matters. And the give and take on a difficult item can sometimes fray nerves rather than build rapport and a cooperative spirit.

Let's look at a negotiation over a bathroom remodeling job. I'm the homeowner, and I want the bathroom overhauled before my prospective mother-in-law comes for a visit next week. You're the contractor, and after a thorough examination you realize the job is going to take five days. I tell you up front it has to be done right away. You say, "Well, I can do that, but it means that I'll have to reschedule my other jobs and take on another helper." Are you willing to accept that in your price?

If I want to get the marriage off on the right foot, I'm stuck, and I've let the contractor know it. By focusing on my needs—my demand—the contractor can add other terms as well: "I can do it quickly, but I need to be able to start at 6 a.m., which means I need coffee for the crew and doughnuts and . . ." You get the general idea. Now I still have a Plan B, of course, but my up-front need has shaped the negotiation and the eventual deal.

MACs VERSUS DELICIOUS

Then there's the opposite approach: Keep the sticky issues until the very end of the process.

You see this as a mutual strategy a lot in local labor negotiations, where the sides put off the difficult issues while they work out simpler matters. The hired guns negotiating the contract between the local teachers union and the board of education may spend a few weeks figuring out whether students should bring Macintosh apples or Delicious on Teacher Appreciation Day before tackling the health plan. This is different than one side holding off talking about the deal breaker, since it's a mutual decision. What the negotiators are generally doing is trying to get a good read on the other side. They may not have dealt with each other's negotiating team before; talking about relatively trivial matters gives them an opportunity to gather information about each other's styles.

Of course, it also allows the other members of their team to gather intelligence and decide on the push. Delay sometimes is not so much a tactic as a signal that one side or the other is not ready to negotiate.

Macs are better, by the way, though if you really want a good apple, hunt up a McCoon.

BACKSIDE DEAL BREAKERS

The true opposite of the up-front deal breaker is the backside deal breaker, which one side rolls out after the other issues are settled, just before the closing phase. Used as a tactic, it's most effective—I should say, thought to be most effective—when the deal is almost in sight: "Okay, now that we've got a price on that bathroom renovation, I need you to do it by next week."

The idea behind the strategy is basically this: By waiting until the very end of the process, the negotiator has allowed the other side to become emotionally involved or attached to the deal. The negotiator has piled up the incentives. The contractor sees he's going to make a nice hunk of change for smacking down a few dozen tiles and parking some nice brass over the sink. He's started to figure what he's going to do with the profit: that ski trip the wife has been pushing for since last year. He now has every incentive to agree to the deal.

But there are downsides for the negotiator using this tactic. For one, introducing a deal breaker after the other points of a deal have been lined up risks scuttling agreement on those other points. And if the other side realizes that the last-minute point is very important, then he can easily use it as leverage: getting attached to deals works both ways.

TELLING FLUFF FROM STUFF

How do you know what's a real deal breaker and what's not?

You use that all-important negotiator's tool: the ear.

Now just because someone says something is a deal breaker doesn't mean it truly is—though I have to admit, that is a strong clue. Hostage negotiators are trained to listen to the subject's rap and see which points they keep returning to. If a subject keeps mentioning that he wants to see his mom, then obviously that's something important to him. (Which by the way doesn't mean he's going to see her. Contrary to TV images, hostage takers' families are rarely brought into negotiations. There are plenty of circumstances where bringing a family member to the scene is absolutely the worst way to go.)

In doubt? Find out. The written word has a certain power in negotiations, and it can be used even before you get to the contract stage or closing. You don't have to have the other side write something down for you, especially if you're negotiating in person. "Let me just review and write down what's important here so I can discuss it with my boss" will get the other side to focus on what's important. Obviously, you can adapt the tactic slightly to fit the situation.

DEADLINES

I love deadlines. I jump up and down for deadlines. Deadlines are a negotiator's best friend. A deadline on a negotiation (as opposed to the thing under negotiation) makes it easy to establish rapport: Both sides are working together to beat a common enemy, the clock.

And the closer the deadline looms, the more likely the either side is to start making concessions. It's human nature not to get serious about doing something until a deadline looms.

Hostage negotiators get deadlines from the other side all the time, but so do other negotiators. Labor contracts typically run out on a specific date, a new business hopes to hire all its employees before its doors open, a catering hall has to be found six months before the wedding, and on and on. The key to dealing with a deadline in negotiations is to use it to your advantage. If you can work without your own deadline while the other side has one, you're in a better position because you have no pressure. If you can at least project that you don't have a deadline, you'll come out ahead.

THE LONG HAUL

Hostage negotiators start every negotiation as if it's going to last for hours if not days. As a general rule, we have time on our side, because experience has shown that a hostage taker's resolve tends to wear down as time goes on. There are dozens of reasons. Maybe the most important is the biological urge for preservation. Fanatics tend to get less fanatical as they grow older.

Of course, we can't wait for a five-year-old to grow into a fifty-year-old. Simply being prepared for the long haul doesn't necessarily mean that the negotiations will be successful. You should know going in what time constraints you have, if any. If it's necessary to adjust your goals because of time—if you have to have a deal before the end of the week or you're not eating—then time is part of your goal.

But the truth is: Usually, time isn't important at all.

Say you have to have a deal during your visit to Chicago.

Really? The boss would tear it up if you did it over the phone at the airport on the way back?

If you're going to buy a new car, does it really matter if you have it this week or next month? If the teachers' contract expires at midnight July 1, what will happen?

FOR REAL, AND NOT

Usually in hostage situations, deadlines are given by the subjects to make it look as if they're coming from a position of power: "I'm going to kill two people at noon if you don't have a car outside." Many times the deadline is mentioned once, and then never comes up again.

Again, the most important tool for determining what is a real deadline, and what's not, are a negotiator's ears. Just as she does with demands, she has to listen to see if the subject focuses on the deadline by mentioning it again and again. Is the hostage taker dedicated to the deadline? Or has he totally forgotten about it?

I have to admit, there's a bit of an art to that, since there's no absolutes. If I feel that a subject is dedicated to the deadline and the negotiations are going nowhere, I tell the commander to get Plan B ready. In a hostage situation that means getting the tactical squad ready. In everyday negotiations, when the other side is dedicated to the deadline and you don't have a basis for an agreement, then you do have to be ready for your out.

READING THE OTHER SIDE'S DEADLINE

In everyday negotiations, deadlines *can* tell you a lot about the other side's positions. Of course, deadlines aren't necessarily presented as deadlines. Sometimes they're sweetened a bit so they look like incentives. You walk into the model of a condo development, and the saleswoman greets you at the door. "We're having a special this month only," she says. "If you buy before Monday, you'll pay only $500,000."

Aside from telling you that housing prices are way out of whack, the saleswoman has given you a price parameter—and one that extends beyond Monday. Now it's possible that something really is going to happen on Monday that will change everything. And it's also possible that someone else will buy the house in the meantime. But in that situation the customer really should ask himself what would happen if he showed up Tuesday morning with $500,000 in hand. Would he be turned away?

But let's say the deadline is real, or at least a soft one, and your research shows that the saleswoman has an incentive to close a deal by Monday. You either do some sleuthing on your own, or the saleswoman keeps coming back to it again and again, which makes you ask why she wants to close that quickly.

And she tells you. Why wouldn't she, if she wants to make the sale and the deadline is in fact real? Failing to answer is the same as admitting that the deadline isn't real, which presumably she doesn't want to do.

Her incentive may not be big—maybe she can't stand this particular model and would like to be done with it. But in sales situations especially, managers often use time periods to motivate their staff: Sell so many widgets or condos by the end of the month and you get to go Hong Kong. More ominous for the salesman are the quotas: Sell so many widgets by the end of the month or you're out of here. Quotas and artificial deadlines are especially popular in auto sales, where things like monthly finance charges can put pressure on management to move product.

So *she* owns the deadline. It's her problem, something you can use to help her reach a successful resolution.

Like getting real and selling you that condo for a price a working man can afford.

Someone else's deadline is just that—someone else's deadline. Let it put pressure on the other side to deal. As the clock winds down, the other side will feel more and more pressure to settle. While you, of course, should be feeling no pressure at all.

A TRICK TO RELAX

How do you avoid pressure in the face of a deadline?

Some people just don't feel pressure at all, no how, no way. Those people live in the cemetery, and the dutiful among us visit them every so often and pay our respects.

The rest of us *do* feel pressure; the trick is controlling it.

Everybody has their own method of dealing with pressure, blowing off steam, and whatnot. When it comes to negotiating deadlines, one thing that works is visualization. Rather than visualizing total disaster—a usual mental image conjured up by the mere mention of the word *deadline*—focus on something else. You can think about your Plan B if you have to . . . or maybe the beer you'll have at the end of the day.

Myself, I like to divert the pressure momentarily; it helps me refocus. Here's what I mean. Throughout the day during particularly stressful negotiations we take breaks. Sometimes these breaks are called for by our subject, and sometimes by us. For the negotiating team, the breaks follow a regular pattern. First we do a roundtable; everyone on the team gets a chance to voice his or her opinion and suggestions, review what's going on, etc.

With that done, I totally detach myself from the incident—and take the rest of the team with me. Maybe I tell a funny story about something odd or strange that happened to me or someone else there or just someone I know. It's amazing to see the tension decrease when we get a moment to laugh about something not related to the situation.

THE FUNNEL

Some negotiations involve only a few issues—and often just one, such as price. Others may involve a whole host of things. If you're negotiating a commercial lease, for example, price per square foot is only one factor, and may not even be as important as included amenities, improvements, lease terms—you get the picture. In building its strategy *before* the negotiation, the team should have attempted to scout the entire field, identifying the many issues that would have to be negotiated. In deciding on its tactics, the team also should decide how "wide" to leave the field.

There's a tendency for negotiations to narrow down into a funnel, leaving the harder points toward the end. Earlier, I mentioned how agreement at an early stage helps build rapport for the tougher spots toward the end. That's the top part of the funnel. When the snags start coming—when you're a thousand dollars apart on the car, or maybe a half dollar on the lease footage—that's the funnel.

Negotiating the points in the funnel is, by definition, the toughest part of the deal. You give me this, I'll give you that, helps some people reach an agreement. So some teams will either:

a.   Hold back a few "gimmes" during the earlier process as bargaining chips in the funnel, or

b.   Revisit some of the earlier points, bringing them up again.

I understand why people do this, but I have problems with both *a* and *b*.

Let's deal with *b* first. If you start revisiting things, you're inviting the other side to do so as well. That may not be fatal—and shouldn't be—but it tends to undermine what you've done to that point, and at the very least it's going to increase the negotiating period. (Of course, if you've made a mistake earlier, you do want to correct it.)

My disagreement with *a* is a little more subtle. Since my negotiations depend on rapport, I prefer to "bank" trust in the early stages. Psychologically, this gives me more leverage as we reach the narrow point of the process. But I admit, I'm very comfortable with being stubborn and saying no. Just as important, I point out what a great, easygoing guy I've been in the early stages, already agreeing to everything the other side wants. The funnel "gimmes" become chits on my side, even if they weren't very important issues for me to begin with. The key to my strategy, of course, is my willingness to stick to my position and take the out if I have to. Personally, I don't think that's any easier if I have a small point to trade in exchange, but some people do. The key is to realize that you're messing with tactics here—NOT your goals.

SUMMING UP

Demands and deadlines make most people nervous. They shouldn't. In most instances, they help good negotiators move together toward a win-win conclusion.

Separate real demands from BS. Ask yourself: What is the other guy focusing on? What topics does he keep coming back to?

Deal breakers can be dealt with at the beginning or the end of the negotiating session—it's up to you.

Don't let the other guy's negotiating deadline become your deadline. It's not.

CHAPTER 9

SOMETIMES IT ONLY TAKES THREE CIGARETTES

The end game:
closing the deal.

Negotiations always have their own individual flow; no two are exactly alike. Still, many of them, maybe even all of them, follow the same general pattern: They go on and on and on, talking talking talking, until at last you end with maybe one or two little nagging points as the last hurdles. They're the last little points you need to clear out to reach an agreement.

Did I say little? Most times they're big, at least in the minds of the people involved in the negotiations. They're stumbling blocks, deal breakers that are the final obstacles to an agreement. Maybe it's price: Isn't $35,000 really too much to pay for a new pickup truck? Maybe it's an amenity: Shouldn't there be a fireplace in the master bathroom suite? Maybe—often—it's something you didn't anticipate being an issue when you sat down at the table: How exactly should the liability clause in the new contract be worded?

That last hurdle can be the worst. It's the doorway at the far end of the hall—the one on the other side of the alligator pit. You can see the ending in sight, you know what you need to do—but, bust a gut, getting past those snapping jaws of death is going to take some serious vine swinging.

Why?

Exactly.

You need to look at the alligator pit—the last hurdle, the hang-up point, the deal breaker, the stumbling block—whatever you want to call the thing that's keeping you from an agreement, and ask: "Why?"

"CLOSING" DEFINED

Time out for half a second to clarify our terms here: The closing of a negotiation is simply the point when you're looking at the very last one or two major issues preventing you from agreeing. In contract situations, the word *closing* can mean something different.

If you've ever bought a house, you know that the closing is that airless moment when you've run out of checks in your checkbook and know you'll have to run to the bank in the morning with your credit cards to cover the overdrafts. In a sales deal, the word *closing* sometimes refers to the handshake at the end, when you get the client to sign on the dotted line. As a negotiator, however, I look at the closing as clearing that last hurdle. As my foot clears that hurdle, I stick out my hand and say, "Great, we've got a deal." I see that end result as part of the process, and that's how I'm dealing with it here.

A SMOKE FOR A LIFE

A few years back, I was involved in a negotiation with a would-be burglar who'd been surprised and then trapped inside an apartment in New York. He had a hostage with him, which of course greatly complicated matters.

Under ordinary circumstances, hostage negotiators find that career criminals—and believe me, crime for this fella was no hobby—are almost always the easiest to deal with. These folks are pros, they know how the system works, and they're generally interested in cutting their losses and getting on with things. I don't doubt that a number of them have better lawyers than I do, but that's another story altogether.

Anyway, the session went along somewhat slowly. We went around a bit, and after a while we got to the point where he was willing to let his prisoner go and surrender. But he got hung up on the ego thing. What I mean is, he wanted to save face and say that he'd gotten something out the cops. I don't know what kind of status that gave him inside of Riker's Island prison, but it soon became clear that it was really important to him. He may have started in with silly demands—I forget now, but they were probably along the lines of a car or something outrageous. He worked down and must've said something about smokes, or maybe I mentioned a cigarette, and before I knew it we were talking about whether he could have a carton of cigarettes. This was back in the days before Mayor Bloomberg and the antismoking mafia banned cigarette smoking from all public places in the city, so cigarettes were not off the table during a negotiation. I told him I couldn't get a carton of cigarettes.

He said a pack.

We didn't have a pack.

"Three cigarettes, then. Give me three cigarettes, and then I'll release the lady."

Frightening what some people think other people's lives are worth, but let's not digress.

"We might be able to do three cigarettes," I told him. "Let me talk to the commander. I'm not the decision maker."

"Three cigarettes, Dom," he said. "Three cigarettes and she walks."

"*And* you come out."

"I throw the gun out and do everything you say."

Now look, that is not a bad deal. That is a *good* deal. That is a winner of a deal. You have a woman who's been locked up for hours, bad guy with a rap sheet longer than my arm, and a gun with enough bullets to end two lives and at least four others. Three cigarettes is a very good deal. I say so, you say so, the whole world says so.

The whole world except for the commander, who vetoed it when I laid it out.

"No way."

"Uh?"

I'm eloquent when I'm baffled, truly I am.

"We have a rule. We never give the suspect something first," said the commander. "He's got to release the hostage. Then we'll give him the cigarettes."

WHAT'S IMPORTANT?

Actually, that was the FBI's rule. I don't want to say that it's a bad rule; it can be a very good rule. At times. Just not this time. Because the hostage taker didn't actually want the cigarettes; he wasn't shaking from some superserious nicotine fit, and he wasn't making a political statement. The cigarettes were important because they would let him say he won something from the police. He made them meet his demands first.

Was it crazy?

Who cares? We're talking about three stinking cigarettes! For a life.

Let me rephrase that calmly and in the proper context: THREE @#$#$%@#$ CIGARETTES!!!!!!!!!!!!!!!

That's all we needed to close the deal. Rather than going over and pulling out a rulebook, what needed to be done there was ask one simple question: Why?

All right, if you want other questions, try these on: What's important? Are the cigarettes important? Is our looking tough important? Is his being able to smile at himself in the mirror important?

Or is the woman's life important?

Why? Because he wants to say he won. If he says that, we get past the alligators, we hit Concept 51, we get a deal.

I explained that to the commander in my most calm, reasonable, businesslike voice. Well, maybe not calmly. And, uh, maybe with a few more words than I have written here. They were very short words. I don't believe any of them had more than one syllable or four letters.

But the boss was the boss. I got back on the phone and told the bad guy the deal was off.

He used a lot of the words I used earlier. After I calmed him down—he was threatening to use the gun, and it took a bit to get him unwound—I eventually promised to go back and take another shot at it with the commander. I have to say that at this point probably the fact that I had been talking with the guy for so long helped a great deal, because the length of time let us build up something of a rapport. The other thing I had going for me was the fact that the guy *did* want to make a deal, as long as he could tell himself he had made it on his terms.

So I went back to the commander, who had been listening to the explosion and realized that he'd almost blown it big-time. Actually, he *had* blown it big-time, but now he had a chance to redeem himself. The commander took a breath, squinted a bit, then said something like, "You know, it's only three cigarettes. Let's give it a shot."

Three cigarettes, one freed hostage, one burglar in custody without shots fired.

And the stinking guy didn't even smoke.

EYES ON THE PRIZE

The commander had committed one of the worst gaffs you can make at any stage in a negotiation, but one that is absolutely fatal at the closing. He forgot to focus on his goal, and instead shifted his attention to his tactics.

Let's call it Dominick's Rule of Eyes on the Prize:

Focus on the result, not the cigarettes or patter that gets you there.

Or another way of putting it: Be flexible in your tactics, but firm in your goal.

Ideally, as the negotiation works down to those few last points at the closing, the other members of the team should be in a position to step back and see what's been achieved and what's left to talk about. Ideally, a break should be scheduled for a review, and the commander should physically remove himself to a quiet space and review the situation. (I can hear some of you thinking, Hey, Tahiti's nice this time of year.) Realistically, the scope of the negotiation may not allow you to call a long time-out, let alone hop a plane for the South Pacific. The important thing is to step back, examine what's already been agreed to, what the hang-ups are, and review the goal. The goal should be tantamount.

EGO TIME

In my experience, egos are most dangerous at closing time. When the negotiation stretches endlessly before you, it's easier to keep your emotions in check. You may be naturally aggressive, but at the start of a negotiation you're usually rested and fresh off a planning session. Your coach is at the top of his game, with good advice that you're willing to take. The commander has told his two really bad jokes only twice apiece, and you're not sick of them yet. The coffee hasn't burned a hole in your gut.

Five, six, twenty hours down the road, you're in no mood to hear those lousy jokes again, and the intel guy smells like a wet fish. The person on the other side of the negotiation, meanwhile, thinks that you've won the entire negotiation. He doesn't buy the negotiating is a win-win thing at all. He wants to get to *yes,* and then some. The last issue often has nothing to do with the cigarettes or the exact payout schedule on the lease; it's macho ego.

You have to keep your perspective throughout the whole negotiation. Forget about winning and losing. You do that on the football field, or playing poker, or if you're really into it, running marathons. Perspective is necessary throughout.

Dividing the team up can help you maintain it. The coach is supposed to watch out for the ego games the negotiator may slip into. The commander is supposed to be above ego, focused on the goal of the negotiation, eyes on the prize. The other team members, not as involved in the give-and-take, can supply a more distant perspective.

One-man teams can have a really hard time with ego. It's not easy to realize it's potentially a problem, or even to know that the other side can use your ego against you. Step back, physically if possible, and run down your goal and the agreements so far. Use the scribe's notes—the paper you started with outlining your goal, the agreements you've recorded—to help you maintain your perspective.

THE FLIP SIDE: EGOS CAN BE USEFUL

Knowing that egos often come out of the closet at the very end can help a negotiator. In the cigarette situation I mentioned above, it didn't take a rocket scientist or a shrink to realize that the hostage taker wanted to save face. That gave me something I could work with. I didn't give in right away—no carton of cigarettes, even though someone could have run down to the corner and gotten one. Why not? Because then it wouldn't have helped him save face. By the time we were done talking on the point, three cigarettes meant more to him than the carton would have—he had *worked me* into an agreement. In his mind, he's wrestled me and won.

That's a loss I'll take every time. Because I keep score by reaching my goal.

The other person's ego can be very useful when you're trying to overcome the last hang-up or two. I don't tell him he's a great negotiator: I let him prove it. I figure out what he wants, then I let him get it from me—in exchange for what I want. If I do *x*, will you do *y*? What about *z*?

Doesn't have to be one for one, but there has to be give-and-take. I find that process helps support the other guy's ego—and probably mine—a lot more effectively than standing there and saying, "You are one fantastic human being."

Which in the situations I deal with is almost never true.

CODDLE THE CHILL

When we first started talking about writing this book, I considered devoting an entire chapter to the need to stay cool under fire. I truly think it's the most important element of successful negotiation. The problem is, there's not all that much to write about. The chapter would have gone something like this:

Stay cool.

Stay really *cool.*

No, I'm serious—stay very cool.

It *is* what you have to do, but it's also the sort of thing you can't learn how to do by me telling you to do it. Staying cool during negotiations is a little like staying cool under fire: You really don't know what's going to work for you until you've been there. And all the advice and checklists in the world are useless if they don't match your own personal style.

But staying cool *is* important. And it's usually when the door is in sight and all you have left are the alligators that it becomes almost impossible. I think maybe if I were into Zen, I could come up with a fancy one-mind-fits-all koan to clear the emotional clutter from your mind at the moment of crisis. But I'm not a Buddhist, and if I were, I would have already come up with a koan that would make me rich. So the best I can do is throw out a few things that help me remain relatively calm when I'm staring down the barrel of a gun:

- *Laughter is the best medicine.* Thank you, *Reader's Digest.* But a sense of humor really does help you stay loose as the ratchets get tightened. Joking can help break the ice with the other side during a negotiation, though frankly, it's the sort of thing that if you have to think about, it isn't going to work for you.

- *The power of pizza.* No, it's not a metaphor for life. It's a literal reminder that you have to feed yourself and keep up your fluids during an all-night

146

or all-day or whatever negotiating session. Now don't go getting cranked on coffee or too relaxed on booze; caffeine will make you even more uptight, and alcohol will make you agree to just about anything. But as we said in Chapter 2, "Position Is Everything," negotiating is a physical as well as a mental process, and it's important to remember that when the body gets hungry, it starts kicking up a fuss. Our bodies were designed hundreds of thousands of years ago when hunger-induced stress was a good thing; it got us out of our trees and into the hunt. It was very useful then and can be useful today, but it tends to distract the mind during a negotiation. Eat, drink, and negotiate.

- *Time-out.* R&R is one of the most underused tactics in business negotiation today. Think about it. How many corporate bosses have walked up to their negotiation team and said, "You guys have a big negotiation coming up next week. Better get ready for it—here are some tickets to the Riviera"?

  Not gonna happen. But it should, and not just because I want to be on the negotiating team that gets those tickets. The mind needs occasional breaks to remain sharp. It's the way God put it together. Teams often take vacations *after* a tough negotiation to celebrate and relax. That's good; we need time to unwind. But in a lot of cases the negotiation would have gone smoother and easier if the team hadn't pulled two back-to-back all-nighters right before jetting out to L.A. for the marathon negotiating sessions.

Breaks in the middle of negotiations are also important. If you can, do something that has zero to do with negotiation or the situation you're dealing with. And I don't mean pulling out the cell phone and arguing with your spouse. Tell jokes, argue sports—better yet, get out and play some hoops, take a walk—the more you can use your body and mind in a completely different way, the more effective the break will be.

Hostage negotiators have breaks in their sessions all the time. I used them first to have a roundtable with everyone, figuring out what was up, making sure we were all on the same page. Once that was done, I'd tell a funny story about something that happened to me, something ridiculous, anything—get a few laughs going. Breaking the tension, enforcing a little R&R, even if only for a few seconds, helped a great deal.

HATE IS A FOUR-LETTER WORD

I guess there's probably nobody in today's society that is worse than a child abuser. Being in close proximity with them can stress you out of your mind.

So how do you deal with them?

As professionally as possible.

I've mentioned this before and I'll mention it again: You try to remove your emotions from the situation. Hostage negotiators deal with real lowlifes all the time; it's most of what we do. Look, I hate these scumbags, but the guy I hate has got an eighty-four-year-old woman by the neck. If I express my hate or even let it influence me, what's going to happen to her?

Hostage negotiators who start to have trouble with the kind of person they're talking to refocus by thinking about the hostage. That's really nothing more than looking at the goal of the negotiation, rather than the person across the table. I'm going to guess that it'll be a lot easier to do in business, where the person on the other side of the table probably hasn't committed a felony.

As a general rule, *any* mental image that creates tension is not useful to the negotiation. That not only includes your opinion of the person you're talking with, but doomsday scenarios of what's going to happen if you fail.

I'm not saying denial is the best way to deal with a negotiation or life. I'm saying that not getting distracted from the goal gives us a much better chance of achieving it.

QUASHING THE DEAL

Here's a little story with the names changed and the circumstances slightly altered to protect the innocent.

Friend of mine was offered a pretty sweetheart deal on a movie option for something that he had been involved in, kind of a life-story thing. Now this was a real starry-eyed time, with people blowing kisses at him and saying the kinds of things that he dreamed of hearing all his life. He went and got himself an agent to do the negotiating with the Hollywood studio that had made the offer. Believe it or not, there wasn't really that much back and forth. The way these things work in real life is that the deal basically has two parts: A little money up front that lets the studio think about it, and a lot more money if the movie is made. Definitions of "little" vary widely—anywhere from a dollar to six figures and beyond.

My friend's offer was, alas, only four figures. And not very big ones.

Which kind of got under his skin, because, like the rest of us, he saw this as a dream come true and the ticket to the good life and yadda-yadda-yadda. Now you can point out that he wasn't being realistic, and I guess you'd be right. I'd point out that how many of us finding ourselves in that situation would be realistic?

But okay, he tosses it around, discusses it with the *real* commander—his wife—and tells the agent to go ahead and cut the deal.

There's a bit of a lag between the oral agreement and the contract—lawyer stuff, I guess—and when the contract gets there, the terms are off by roughly $100.

"What's this?" says my friend.

"Those are the expenses to cover the FedEx and fax fees."

"FedEx and fax? What FedEx and fax?"

The agent explained that some documents had changed hands and the charges for them had been deducted from the sum offered.

"I have to pay for that? After they took six months to send me the contract? And now they're going to take another six months to pay me, and gyp me besides? No way."

Now as a matter of fact, my friend happened to have been right—ordinarily those are considered regular costs of doing business, and the person on the other side of the deal pays them out of pocket. But there were special circumstances involved, and somewhere along the way, the agent had agreed to it, thinking it was a minor hurdle.

And it was. Except to my friend. From his perspective, he was being nickeled-and-dimed to death. He hadn't gotten what he was worth in the first place, his agent was going to take a cut, the lawyer was taking a cut, and even the FedEx guy was getting more than he was.

Yeah, I know, the FedEx guy wasn't. But no one—including his agent—could convince him of that. The deal died. You've never seen the movie about my friend, because it never even got past the discussion stage.

EXPLAINING THE SURRENDER

Some people would say that my friend's ego got in the way of the deal. I'd have to agree, of course, but I think the agent was the one who was really at fault. He didn't explain about the charges properly. If he had, my friend would have had a better perspective on them. In hostage negotiator's terms, the agent *closed* okay, but then failed to *explain the surrender*. He should have told my friend about the charge, clearly. But he also should have told him how long the contracts would take to be prepared, which clearly irked my friend.

In a hostage situation, the first few minutes are usually the most dangerous for the hostages, since things are very volatile. There's all sorts of energy flowing. Things have gone wrong already, and one little mistake can be magnified exponentially. Not that I would call any moment when you're held at gunpoint a picnic, but things tend to calm down a bit after that first adrenaline rush. Then comes the *next* most dangerous time: the moment the bad guy comes out from behind the barricades to surrender.

Think about it: He's got a gun, he's nervous as hell, the ninjas have guns, and they're nervous as hell too. They claim they're not nervous, but they're nervous. I was one, I know. One little screw-up, boom. In a hostage situation the surrender is always complicated because trust is never going to be at 100 percent—we've had to work hard just to get it to 51 percent, as we discussed earlier. The police have to be prepared for the worst-case scenario:

Yes, the bad guy has agreed to surrender peacefully.

Should we trust him?

Never.

Bad guys have been known to lie. A number of them over the years have agreed to surrender peacefully and at the very last minute started a shootout with the police. This is known as suicide by cop—the person actually wanted to die but did not have the balls to do it himself.

On the other side of the law, the hostage taker or barricaded individual has no reason to trust the police. Yes, the negotiator has made all kinds of promises that they will not be harmed. Every promise until now that was made had been kept. But that was in the past. Maybe it was a clever trick. Those people out there have guns, a lot of them.

That's why AFTER we have a deal, after we've moved past the closing, hostage negotiators always go over the surrender very carefully. This is what you have to do, this is what's going to happen, this is what the steps are. One, two, three. The hostage taker can even get a little annoyed at this point. "I know all this," he may say. He wants to sign on the bottom line and get it over with.

I go over it very slowly, step-by-step. We don't want any surprises.

In our business, one of the best tactics we use to handle the surrender is a simple one: We slow things down and go step-by-step. I have had ranking officers who hear that our subject wants to surrender and say, "Good, lets get him out of there right away." Although I understand their rush to end the situation, I have at times had to assert myself by pointing out to them that this was the time to slow things down. This is the time to make sure all t's are crossed and i's are dotted. We outline everything with the hostage taker and make sure our own people are ready to rock.

NO SURPRISES

Surrender is not the right word to use to describe what happens after the closing in an everyday deal, but the idea of avoiding surprises should be exactly the same. You have an agreement, but it's a fragile agreement. Very possibly there will be a time lag between your handshake and the formal contract, if one is required. (Let's ignore the question of what sort of contract that handshake represents, since we're not lawyers.) A lot of things can happen in that time that you can't control or even know.

The one thing that you *do* know is that you won't be there to go over the points slowly and calmly with the person on the other side of the negotiation. The rapport that you've developed over several hours or days of negotiation will have grown cold. So you're doing yourself a big favor by reviewing not only the important points of the contract, but the exact next steps that will take place: You'll arrange to have an inspector look over the property, a mortgage will be obtained, yadda, yadda, yadda.

That's a two-stage review:

1. The terms

2. What will happen next, whether it's part of the agreement or not

If you haven't done both, you haven't finished the negotiation.

SUMMING UP

Sooner or later every negotiation hits the end game—the last two or three points between you and the deal.

With the goal in sight, tension can rise. This is the time to keep your cool. Whether you're a Zen Buddhist or a city cop who plays killer basketball to relax, program in some quick down time to keep cool.

Egos are always a problem, but they can be killers at the closing. Be alert—not just for yours, but for your opposite number's. Feed it if it helps.

In hostage situations, the surrender is one of the most dangerous times of all. In everyday negotiations, take a tip from the hostage people—don't allow your opposite number to be surprised.

CHAPTER 10

THE FIVE-MINUTE CAR DEAL AND MORE REAL-LIFE ADVENTURES

A hostage negotiator looks at some real-life negotiation problems.

Once upon a time there was a man who wanted to buy a car. Nothing too fancy—it was your basic, everyday family sedan. He took out a piece of paper, folded it in half, and then wrote out what he absolutely needed and what he wanted. He thought hard—really hard—about how much he could afford and where the money would come from. He then began going through car magazines to see what the possibilities were. He narrowed his choices down to three vehicles, then did some research on car prices.

Along the way he discovered that sticker prices are actually several thousand dollars more than invoice prices—in other words, he saw that dealers pay one price, the invoice, and then put another, the sticker, on the car. Thanks to the Internet, he had no problem getting a ballpark figure on what the three cars he was looking at would actually cost the dealer. He knew that his numbers didn't include some of the discounts that the dealer also obtained, but he nonetheless had a rough idea of the dealer's cost going in. Realizing that the dealer had to make some money on the sale, he did a bit more research and was able to get a realistic idea of a fair price for each vehicle. In this case, it worked out almost exactly to $500 more than the invoice, after a series of other incentives were subtracted.

He then went for some test drives in the cars, carefully saying he was just looking and getting a feel for what he wanted. The test drives helped him prioritize his wish list. They also gave him an idea of what the different dealerships were like, and reinforced what he had heard about how sales of the particular models were going. At the car lot stocked with Brand X, he was just about knocked over by salesmen in the empty showroom when he walked in the door. Looking at Brand Z, in contrast, he practically had to shout to get any attention.

The research done, he made his plans and went forth to negotiate. He went to the dealer—Brand Y, as it turned out—found the salesman who had arranged for his test drive, and sat down at his desk.

"I want to buy a Brand Y," he told him. "I want the car. I'm ready to buy, and I want to do it today—actually, in the next fifteen minutes. I'm willing to pay this."

"This" was the fair price he had determined earlier.

The salesman blinked a second, then started on some spiel he'd been taught during his job orientation training six or seven months before.

"No, here's the thing," said the buyer. "I want to buy, but I only have fifteen minutes. I'll pay this."

The salesman blinked again, then excused himself, got up and went to talk to the sales manager. The deal was done within fifteen minutes.

WHY DID IT WORK?

That once-upon-a-time story is actually the way I've bought almost all of my cars. I think it illustrates some of the hostage negotiation principles in a real-life way with something we're just about all going to do at some point in our lives. It's a good model for a basic, real-life negotiation. So let's run through it quickly, and you can draw your own conclusions about what'll work for you.

First of all, the key to any deal is knowing what you want. My needs for a vehicle are pretty straightforward, and I'm not into status. That means the vehicles I want to buy are not necessarily the "hottest" models or the luxury ones with sexy markups. It also means that I can move from a Chevy to a Ford to a Toyota pretty easily. Now you may think that makes the negotiations easy, but the fact is, there's *always* something you're not going to budge on, some goal that's difficult to meet—the price, for example. While it's true that you may have more choices at a certain price level, those choices only make it emotionally easier for you to walk away from one particular situation. They don't affect the specific negotiations.

Got that? As long as you have an *out*—the choice to say no—you are in a strong position. It makes no difference what the out is—two hundred other car models or a pair of in-line skates—the out is the out is the out. If your goal isn't met, you take your out.

I didn't start negotiating for a car until I was ready to negotiate—I did all of my intelligence work, set my goals, knew my strategy. The negotiation didn't begin during a test drive. It happened long afterward; several weeks, in fact.

Assessing the situation and planning my negotiations tactics, I decided there was no call for a lot of back-and-forth. I knew I wanted the car, and I had no problem paying a fair price for it. I wasn't interested in macho games of winning points during negotiation; I can't drive ego through the car wash. On the salesman's side, there wasn't a lot of cause for back-and-forth either—Brand Y only came with certain options, and I knew precisely what I wanted. He wanted to sell the car. The only question—the only one—was whether he would sell it at that price.

So I went to the salesman, said clearly that I was ready to buy, and made him an offer. I knew it was fair; I didn't know whether he would take it or not.

What was the fifteen minutes for? It had nothing to do with my needs; the car I was driving would last indefinitely. And it actually wasn't a real deadline for him either—I could use it to leave, of course, but if we were filling out paperwork at sixteen minutes past the hour I wasn't going to say, "Sorry, you blew it."

I was signaling to him that I was serious. I told him I *did* want to buy the car: "Here's the money. Let's not screw around. Let's do the deal." It's a bit of a gimmick to get his attention, but the checkbook I pulled from my pocket probably worked just about as well.

As a one-man negotiator, my team system and feedback was very simple: The commander gave his approval only if the price was met. Anything else would have caused me to walk out and reset my strategy. That was another benefit of the fifteen-minute deadline: I could avoid a drawn-out process that would have just wasted time.

Could I have gotten the car for $300 over invoice instead of $500? For $200? For $400? For $499?

Who knows? Who cares!

I reached my goal and got my car. You don't second-guess yourself once the hostages are freed and the bad guy is in the jail.

WIGGLE ROOM

One of the keys to the car negotiation I just described is the fact that the price I give is actually my goal; it's as non-negotiable as the shade of black on the model in question. I believe it's easier to simply state the goal right out; there's less time wasted. The other side in a car deal has done the same thing by presenting a specific set of options and models for sale. They've limited the universe, so why can't I?

The one practical difficulty with this method is that many people are not going to take you at your word when you say up front that you're making your final offer, at least not when money is involved. I don't think that's an argument against doing it; on the contrary. But you do have to indicate that you really, truly mean it.

Like I said, that's the idea of the deadline. But I have to say, from experience, that you'll be tested.

Not a problem, right? Because you can always take your out.

Some negotiators want a little wiggle room to work with, even in a very simple negotiation. They'll make a money offer a little lower than their goal, knowing they're likely to come up a bit to make the deal. Negotiation is an art, not a science; you do what you're comfortable with, as long as it meets your goal. Remember, though, that giving yourself wiggle room involves *tactics,* NOT—repeat, NOT—your goal. Your goal always remains steadfast.

COMPLICATIONS

A negotiation to buy a car is a good real-life example not only because we all do it, but also because it parallels most situations where we buy something, be it for ourselves or a large corporation. There's a fairly limited range of possibilities, both in terms of possible products and options, and in price. Up-front research and decision making presents the negotiator with a relatively easy task; once the negotiation gets under way, there will generally be only one or two sticking points—one, actually, and it's almost always price. The negotiator can focus his strategy on clearing that last hurdle at the closing. While being realistic and ready to grab your out are often easier said than done, those really are the keys to a good negotiation, especially in a relatively straightforward situation like a car sale.

But what about situations in which there are a ton of hard to quantify variables? Where not only are you dealing with your emotions, but with the other side's as well? And where you have a complicated relationship with your negotiating team—and so does the other side?

In real life, we call that buying a house.

NEEDS AND WANTS

For many of us, buying a house is going to be one of the biggest purchases we ever make. It's also one of the most complicated. Not only is a lot of money involved, but there's the whole question of where you want to live, who your neighbors will be, practical maintenance questions, ego things, emotional attachments—the decision to buy a house can be a real nightmare.

But that doesn't mean the *negotiation* should be.

I happen to have been in this situation myself as I sat down to write this book. I started very simply, sitting down at the kitchen table with a sheet of paper. "Needs" went on one side, "Wants" on the other. I *need* three bedrooms, one for me and the wife, one for the child who still lives with us, another to be used occasionally by the other kids who visit. I *want* five—this way all the kids have their own rooms and we can have guests, I have a bed handy when the wife starts to snore, etc.

I went down the list, room by room, then moved to the outside. Finally I came up with a realistic figure on what I could afford to spend . . . and what I wanted to spend, which obviously was a little less.

I'm not writing a psychology book here, or even one on houses, so I'm not going to get off on a big long tirade about being realistic about money and houses and egos and that sort of thing. And let me tell you this right now: If, like my friend Jimmy, you want to buy an $875,000 house for $350,000, you're going to need more than negotiating skills. I know it's hard to be absolutely realistic, especially these days and especially about houses. The list you start with of needs and wants helps you do that, but obviously the list alone can't keep your emotions in check. The more up-front work you do, the easier it may be . . . but real life is, admittedly, messy.

Once you know what you need and want, you're ready—not to buy the house, not even to look at them, but to pick your negotiating team. Because in this sort of complicated scenario, you (and probably your spouse) are the commander(s). The real estate agent is going to do the real negotiating.

Real estate agents, even so-called "buyer agents," are never really working for you. They're working for their commissions. That's fine; they need to pay their own mortgage and send their kids to school and do all that good stuff you're trying to do too. You can work with them—you can work with anyone, really—as long as you keep that in mind. Their motivation is making their commission, which only happens if they make a deal.

Any deal.

Your motivation is different. Your goal is a certain kind of house at a certain price in a certain neighborhood. Different goal. Very important to remember.

MY INTERESTS

I interview the real estate agents to get an idea of what they're like before I get into the buying process. As I talk to them—and this can happen in their office, at an open house, whatever—I want to see if they'll listen to me. Are they going to take my needs and concerns to heart when they're trying to find me a house and negotiate? Or are they just giving me information they could leave on an answering machine? If they're asking a lot of questions about what I want and going into depth on my needs, then I feel much more confident that they're not going to waste my time by showing me things I don't want or that they'll fail to emphasize what I think is important to the other side. If I tell them something is not what I want, I expect them to remember that and be able to translate it into the next listing I see.

I also want to feel I can trust them to be honest with me. Not to put my interests above theirs—nobody really does that, at least not in a business relationship—but to be honest with me. You have to trust the other members of the team. It's like a long-term relationship in a short period of time. If you don't trust them at the start, where are things likely to go afterward?

Personally, I don't care what kind of negotiator the agent is. I can't really tell until they're involved in the negotiation anyway, and generally it's irrelevant. No, not because I can give them pointers, though obviously

I could if they want. My feeling is that as commander, I can always say no, and that's all the control I need over the negotiations. A great negotiator, a bad negotiator—it's the *goal* I'm focusing on, not their style. Bad negotiators make good deals all the time, and vice versa.

One other thing: If I'm saying no a lot to the negotiator, I made a bad choice about who the negotiator should be in the first place.

INTEL FIRST

So the wife and I go out, trudge through a billion houses, and finally we find one just at the edge of what we want and need. The price is $450,000 rather than the $400,000 we want to pay. Now we're ready to negotiate.

Uh, no, not yet. We need to gather intelligence.

The most common mistake in a complicated negotiation—and you see it in house sales all the time—is to confuse your *decision-making process* with *intelligence gathering*. Knowing roughly how much you want to pay and the number of rooms, etc., has NOT told you anything about the house and what it should be worth. I'm going to focus on money here because it's easier to talk about, but in fact there are usually a whole range of issues involved. You can't negotiate them until you've done your intelligence.

So that's what my next step is. I ask the real estate agent for comparable sales, which shows me price ranges. And I hire a house inspector to look over the property.

I'm going to guess that if you've ever bought a house, you waited until *after* the deal was done to bring on the inspectors. The problem is that by then the information is of much less value to you. Oh sure, maybe you got an adjustment for a few outrageous items, but think of how much more ammunition you would have had if you went into the negotiations with the inspector's report.

To use my $400,000/$450,000 example—let's say, for the sake of discussion, that the inspector's report comes back and says, well, you need a new roof and the dishwasher is *x* years old and this and that and that and this. All told, he comes up with roughly $20,000 worth of items that need attention or at least are worth looking into.

Things to talk about? You bet. And not only do you have intelligence in this case, but you also have a supposed outside party supplying the information, someone you can use to bolster your position. (He's not really an outside party, since you wrote the check, but inspectors are often treated as if they're neutral, for some reason.)

When I make a counteroffer to the other side, I present them with information to back up my position. My inspector has identified these items; I'm going to be out of pocket for them, time involved, etc.—what can you do for me?

By the way, I make it clear I want to buy the house at my price. In my case, my price is *my price,* just as it was in the car negotiation. You may feel more comfortable leaving yourself a little bit of a cushion, but that's not really all that important. As a practical matter, you'll probably end up using that cushion anyway—if it's there, most of us are going to take advantage of it.

CLOSING THE NEGOTIATION

At some point, the seller comes back with a more serious price. In this case, let's say it's $420,000. He throws in a few other things that were on my want list to sweeten the deal, including the nice rug in the living room that the wife loved. Now we're at the closing stage of negotiations; we can see the doorway and the deal. The real estate agents are jumping up and down, the kids are getting antsy, the pressure's on.

Come up with the $20,000? Offer to split the difference?

If you were being realistic when you set your goal of $400,000, no. Your out isn't to pay more; your out is to find another house.

Now, there's nothing wrong with reviewing your process and examining your assumptions and rethinking everything . . . as long as you can completely divorce yourself from the emotions of making the deal (and probably the house). Odds are you can't, which sends us back to the original sheet of paper you drew up. This is the time when you have to have faith in your original process, and your selection of your out. If $400,000 is your limit, that's the way it is.

But the wife really wants the house, and the rug put her over the edge. (She says it's worth five grand. I say I saw one at Home Depot last week for $350.)

My response would be to go to the real estate agent and say, "Look, I understand blah-blah-blah and he's a great guy and that shade of mauve is just so mauve I can't believe it, but—$400,000 is all I can afford. What can you do for me?"

The result is going to be the seller's last, best offer. Don't kid yourself—it's unlikely after that point that the number is going to come down. It's at that point you choose to close the deal or take your out.

GETTING WHAT YOU WANT

The techniques in this book can be almost infinitely adapted to different situations. From what I see, a lot of negotiations fail because of the lack of up-front intelligence. It makes no sense to go in and ask for a raise if you're already being paid more money than everyone else in your field.

Actually, I do think you can do that, as long as you do it right. First of all, don't bring that up . . . and make sure you have a *real* good answer for it when your boss does.

Not: "Well I'm worth more."

Try: "I brought in 50 percent more business to the company than anyone else in the tristate area."

You can get what you want by putting the argument in the most coherent, logical manner possible: not because you're appealing to the other side's sense of fairness, but because you're showing the other side why it's a good deal for them.

Not that guilt doesn't work sometimes. How many salesmen have taken a shot at it by bringing up their kids' education? Probably plenty. If you can play on the heartstrings effectively, go for it.

SPEAKING OF SALESMEN . . .

Since I brought it up, this seems as good a place as any to give you my take on salesmen who tell customers, "I am not making a dime on this sale."

Bull feathers. That is the most ridiculous statement a salesman can make. Another car story close to home: I was doing some research on buying a new vehicle. (This time I ended up with a Chevy Silverado 2500 HD, but that's another story.) One dealership I decided to browse in was a nice, comfortable setting to spend $30,000; free coffee, soft music in the background, very relaxed atmosphere. A young salesman approached me and asked if he could help. I did my usual routine: Told him exactly what I wanted and let him know that he had a very short time to give me the best deal of my life and I would walk out with a new truck and he would walk out with a commission, blah-blah-blah.

So far so good. This guy started using his calculator at 100 mph, then leaned back in his chair and became real sullen. He lowered his voice a few levels and said, "I really should not do this, but I am going to give you the truck for $200 over what you said was your bottom line."

I looked at him and said, "Really? Do you think that's a good deal?"

His voice became even lower. I thought the guy was going to cry. "Yes, it is a great deal. I'm not making a dime off of this sale."

I just started laughing. End of negotiation, end of sale, end of story.

Let's face it: If you can find someone who'll spend all day away from his family and sit in a car dealership and not make any money, I want him to come work for me. My house needs painting, and I don't feel like paying very much.

NO CONS

I'm not above relying on emotional factors to help me negotiate. I can't deny that they work. A friend of mine made sure to bring the kid along when he went with his wife to talk to a surgeon about an operation she was going to undergo. He wanted to subtly remind the surgeon what was at stake. It may not have been a traditional negotiating setting, but the operation did go well.

Guilt trips are fine, and persuading people is what we're all about. But you can't con someone. It comes back to the whole thing about telling the truth.

As I said earlier, the one question new hostage negotiators freeze or stumble on when they're in a negotiation is: "Do I have to go to jail?"

Shit yeah, asshole. And probably for a long time.

The negotiator can't say no; lying is a quick fix, and any savvy person on the other side is going to see it as a con. And saying "I don't know"—which technically is often the "right," true answer—doesn't work, because usually you get an instant reply: "You know I am going to jail."

Instead, when I'm in a situation like that, I say something along the lines of: "Look, here's the deal. I know why you are in there and you know why you are in there, right?" It's a gimme question, one of those "yes" responses that are so important. It's really asking permission to tell the other guy the truth. Because when the bad guy says yes, my response then is along the lines of: "All I can tell you is you have to go through the system. Jail time is totally up to you, your lawyer, and the court. The most important thing I need for you to consider right now is this: What happens at those proceedings is totally in your hands. What you do right now will influence how that turns out."

It's not a lie at all, and in fact the conversation goes on from there.

"Aw, come on, man," the bad guy might say. "You know I'm going to do time."

Again, the truth, this time presented as a question: "Do you know anyone who committed a crime, went to court, and walked without doing any time?"

They answer, inevitably: "Yes."

We'll save our discussion on the American criminal justice system for another time. The point is, I've used the truth to tell them what they don't want to hear, and to build rapport and respect at the same time.

MANIPULATION

I can hear a few objections from the back of the room. "Uh, yo, uh, Dominick—isn't manipulation just a form of lying?"

No.

Next question.

Seriously, the fact that you have to treat someone fairly by *not* lying and *not* conning them doesn't mean that you don't:

- Present the best arguments in *your* favor

- Do what you can to put them in a frame of mind where they'll accept those arguments

I'm not talking about fraud, I'm talking about persuasion. And I think most people can recognize the difference. I'm not expecting the Chevy salesman to tell me the Silverado's *bad* points; I just don't want him to give me out and out BS about his bargaining position. I'm not upholding truth, justice, and the American way—that's Superman's job. I'm just looking for an honest deal. In the case of a car sale, that deal involves not just the vehicle, but the service and maintenance on the vehicle, and the backup if something goes wrong. A dealer who encourages his employees to flat out bullshit like that—well, would you trust them with anything more serious than an oil change?

BRINGING HOME THE BACON

My favorite manipulation story involves Frank Bolz. Now you've probably never heard of Frank, but within the world of hostage negotiation, the man is a god. He was a pioneer and an inspiration for most of us who followed him. There are a bunch of incredible Frank Bolz stories floating around, and they're all true.

Frank had his team up in the city one time, trying to get a hostage taker out of an apartment. It had been a ball-busting night, and now dawn was breaking. He sensed that he just about had the guy out . . . but as we know, that last 1 percent of trust he needed can be the most elusive of all. So he decided he needed to do something to get the guy in the right frame of mind.

What to do, what to do . . .

Frank thought about it for quite a while, as he tells it, and then finally sprang into action. He sent a pretty perplexed young cop to the corner grocery store for a pound of bacon. In the meantime, he found and set up a little propane grill in the hallway outside the barricaded apartment. Within a few minutes of the cop's return, the hallway was filled with the toasty smell of bacon crackling in the pan.

"We're having breakfast out here," Frank told the guy inside. "You oughta come out. . . ."

He did.

THE "I'M YOUR FRIEND" ATTITUDE

Is being nice manipulation?

Yes and no. You definitely do catch more flies with honey than vinegar, and many more deals are made through cooperation and friendship than ill will. I think a little manipulation along those lines is fine. But just a little. Too much is dangerous.

Hostage negotiators deal with people we don't like all the time. Not one of the people I've talked off of bridges or out from behind barricades gets a postcard from me every year. Yeah, it's nice to make friends, and that's what life is all about—but negotiating is not making friends.

In everyday situations, emotions often skew the negotiations. It's not just falling in love with a house or really wanting to impress people with a certain type of car. The emotions involved in talking to someone are part of the swirl. You can deal with them to an extent by focusing on your goals, but it's hard to keep yourself separate.

When I talk to new hostage negotiators, one of the things I emphasize is, "Leave your cop attitude outside." When you're negotiating with a pedophile, you can't think like a cop—because thinking like a cop is going to make you want to march in there and arrest him. At best.

It's the same way with someone you like or would *like* to like on the other side of the negotiating table. Leave your *friend attitude* outside. I'm not saying be a mean person, or even to be cold and distant. Be friendly if that's your style. But focus on your goal. You're negotiating, not having a drink.

All right, you may be having a drink—but it's a tactic and a means to an end, not the reason you're there.

SUMMING UP

Different negotiations call for different tactics, but the overall approach is the same. Divide up the team, decide on your goal and tactics, do your intelligence, negotiate when you're ready.

Simple or complex, you always have to know your role in the negotiation—and trust the other members of your team.

Don't confuse your decision-making process with gathering intelligence about a deal.

Conning someone is not the way to make a deal. But you can and should use the truth to your best advantage.

And finally, nothing will smooth the way to a settlement like a whole bunch of bacon cooking in the hallway.

CHAPTER 11

DON'T GET TAKEN

Tips to avoid becoming a sucker— or a hostage.

Someone recently asked me how to avoid becoming a sucker. I came right back with the only answer I know: *Don't get married.*

Besides some yuks at the expense of my ex-wife, there's a serious point there. Sometimes you *do* get taken, at least a little. Life is life; you can't be so afraid of losing a game here or there that you don't play it. Better to have loved and lost than never loved at all, right?

All right, I'm not sure about that either. But I do think it's better to be in the game than the alternative.

AVOIDING TROUBLE

Early in my career I was part of a special unit that did foot patrols in bad neighborhoods. One night we'd go into Harlem, the next the South Bronx. This was back in the 1970s, and there was no such thing as gentrification at the time. The parts of the city that we went through were war zones, especially at night.

One of the things we would preach to law-abiding people in the areas was to avoid trouble. Very obvious stuff—don't go out very late at night if you don't have to, buddy up, don't walk alone in a darkened ally, things like that. Most of the people who lived there already knew those things; it was part of their common sense. Where they got into trouble was not looking far enough ahead to see that the choices they were making would put them into situations they knew they should avoid. Staying out late at a bar because So-and-so's brother *may* drop by to give you a ride home . . . formula for disaster.

It seems obvious when you put it like that. But how many people find themselves in a situation where they *have* to have a car because the old one just died? Or they have to take whatever apartment at whatever price they can get because the lease on the other one runs out next week?

I know, I know: Life is what happens while you're making plans for something else. If you find yourself up against it—negotiating at the point of a gun—not a problem; this book is for you. But as much as you can, plan ahead. Try to build time into your business and personal situations so that the deadlines are always the other guy's, not yours. Let him walk down the dark alleys, not you.

Whether you're talking about business or a car sale or a date with your girlfriend, if the deal looks too good, best to be suspicious. You can't get something for nothing. If you're buying land cheaper than swampland . . . it's probably swampland with toxic waste. You can be a hell of a great negotiator and still not be able to talk yourself out of a ditch when you're up to your neck in radioactive alligators.

Or to put it another way: When I walked the beat, I carried a gun.

HOW NOT TO BE A HOSTAGE

Probably because of what I do, people often ask me for advice on how not to become a hostage. They mean that literally; these are not the most secure of times.

My usual response is along the lines of, "Do what you usually do." Truth is, there are very few real hostage situations on any given day; most of us will never be taken hostage. And most of those who are, will eventually be released.

That applies to everyday negotiations as well, whether in business or daily life. The fact of the matter is, most negotiations are going to result in a favorable outcome. Most people you deal with are not going to try to score big off you, let alone cheat you big-time. That's not to say they won't try and cut a deal that's advantageous to them. That's only fair—so are you.

I'm not saying you ought to just take what the other side offers the first time around. On the contrary—take only a deal that fulfills your goal. My point is that there are many more honest people in the world than most of us think. And even the people who are only vaguely honest generally cut deals that are in the ballpark.

HOW NOT TO BE BULLIED

But don't be a mark. And don't be a pushover. The more you know about the situation BEFORE you begin negotiating, the better the outcome is likely to be. Know the manufacturer's list price and the invoice price of the new car you want BEFORE you begin to negotiate. Know the options, know your out.

As you negotiate, remember these four things:

1. You're negotiating, not making the final decision. That's the commander's job.

2. Since making the final decision is not *your* job, you can't be forced into doing something you don't want to do. If you feel the other side—be it a negotiator or a salesman or a pushy customer—demanding a decision, simply say, "It's not up to me. I'm just negotiating."

    Or some variation.

3. Negotiation is a personal art. Some people like to shout and do it a lot. Others like to speak very quietly. In my experience, the quiet ones are

the ones who succeed in most negotiations, as long as they stick to their goals and do their homework. But if bustin' a blood vessel works for you, go to town.

4. The easiest thing to do—the thing you can always *always* always do—is take your out. You can always walk away.

WHEN YOU CAN'T WALK AWAY

Actually, that's a lie. There are times when you can't walk out—when you really are the hostage, not the negotiator. Your back was turned and suddenly there are masked men with guns in the lobby of the bank, telling everyone to put up their hands. The ex-boyfriend violates the order of protection and drives through three states to somehow find you. Your mother-in-law manages to hack the code on your Caller ID, and you pick up the phone by mistake.

What do you do?

The first thing to do is also the hardest thing: Stay calm, stay cool. If you're in a position to say something, make whatever you say contribute to calm.

The next thing to do is realize that you are *not* a negotiator; you're a hostage. Hostages are not in a position to negotiate because they're not going to have anything the hostage taker wants. Unless there's a possibility of a transaction, there's no basis for negotiation. Hostages have no out; negotiators do. In order to negotiate, the hostage has to stop being a hostage.

People trapped in a bank with robbers probably are generally not going to be in a position to step out of the hostage role. That's why there are hostage negotiating teams. But a businessman trying to get a new insurance policy, or a young secretary trying to buy a car, or parents trying to get a better education for their children, can. They do it by finding viable alternatives to the present situation. If you can walk out the front door of the bank without being shot, you're not a hostage. If you can get a new insurance policy by taking your business down the street, you're not a hostage. If you can pick and choose between different amenities on the new house, you're not a hostage.

In nearly all negotiations in everyday life, there are options, even if they're not immediately obvious. There's always an out you can take. Knowing that is very powerful. It means you're not a hostage—you can negotiate.

THE NONHOSTAGE MINDSET

Ninjas put on body armor when they go to work. Hostage negotiators put on a lot of the same gear when they have to get up close to the guy with the gun. Everyday negotiators do too. Even better, it's a lot lighter than the Kevlar and not nearly as sweat-inducing.

Your body armor is your mindset. I'm not going to give you a formula; it's yours. I hope my book has influenced you, but at the end of the day, your head is something I can't get into, for physical reasons; you'll have to monkey around in there yourself. But if it helps any, here's my mindset, boiled down to a single sentence:

"Everything can be worked out, as long as we do it together."

I must have said it a zillion times over the past ten years, both in negotiations and in classes. I truly believe it. I think that if I have a problem or, as it more usually goes, someone else has a problem, it can be worked out through negotiation. Talk to me; I'll listen. We'll work it out.

I don't mean that I'm going to "win." I mean that the problem is going to be resolved in a way that is both beneficial to me and to the person on the other side of the situation. It's a positive mindset, no doubt. It may even be a little cocky, given what I do. But it's also realistic. For me, I don't "win" a negotiation by tallying chits or getting the macho rush. I succeed by reaching a reasonable goal.

Like I said, I hope after reading this book that your mindset will be somewhat similar. But only somewhat similar—negotiating is an art, as I've said, not a science. In order to succeed, a negotiator's mindset has to reflect his or her personality. What I've outlined for you are a set of principles that are fairly flexible, I hope very simple, and most important, adaptable to different situations and a wide range of personalities. How you use them is your call.

GUT CHECK

Lists of what to do in a negotiation are great. Books, like this one, that get you thinking about your own methods and the steps you should or shouldn't take are fantastic. You can learn to be a negotiator, and a big part of learning should come from books and lectures and classes.

But sometimes it just comes down to doing it. Even for the pros, negotiation is just a gut check.

When the man who hijacked the Lufthansa jet agreed to surrender, there was one little snag involved. It wasn't a snag, exactly; you might call it a condition, except it wasn't precisely that either. Part of the deal was, the hijacker wanted to surrender to me.

Which, you know, was cool, because I *was* a cop. I did arrest people. It may even have been in my job description.

But I'll tell you, it was a long, long walk out on that concrete. I wore a bulletproof vest, but that doesn't cover every part of your body. One of the downsides to being trained as a sniper is that you're very aware of the parts of your body that aren't covered.

And another thing: Airbus 310s are very large aircraft. Lots of places for people to hide. Guy with a gun near the tail, in the cockpit . . .

The door opened.

We waited.

Man came out.

Came down the steps.

There was a second there, a split split second, when I thought maybe it might all go wrong. I was beyond negotiation at that point—I was beyond trust and any of that stuff. I was just a cold guy on an airport runway, taking a chance on my gut that this was going to work.

And I was scared for that split split second, as scared as I'll ever be.

Then that instant passed and it was over. Ninjas around, good arrest, happy hostages freed, newspapers, TV.

It all looks easy now.

THE HARDEST NEGOTIATION

You take risks every time you go out, no matter whether your negotiation is life and death or for a few extra minutes of break time. Don't let yourself get frozen by fear. Everybody feels it in some situations; it's part of being human. The key is not to get paralyzed by it. If you do, if you don't make the attempt at the negotiation, then you have exactly zero chance of achieving the goal you want.

The most important negotiation you'll ever do is the next one.

It'll also be the hardest.

Good luck with it. I know you'll get through it.

Take care and stay safe.

INDEX

ABOUT THE AUTHOR

Dominick J. Misino is the former primary negotiator for the New York City Police Department. In 1993 he negotiated a nonviolent end to the dramatic hijacking of Lufthansa Flight 592. An internationally recognized expert on business negotiation, he has been featured in the *Harvard Business Review* and on CNN and *Good Morning America,* among other nationally televised programs. He can be reached through his Web site at www.hostagenegotiation.com.